An Introduction to
GLOBAL CITIZENSHIP

An Introduction to
GLOBAL CITIZENSHIP

Nigel Dower

EDINBURGH UNIVERSITY PRESS

Copyright © Nigel Dower, 2003

Edinburgh University Press Ltd
22 George Square, Edinburgh
Transferred to digital print 2006

Typeset in Sabon by
Hewer Text Ltd, Edinburgh, and
printed and bound in Great Britain by
CPI Antony Rowe, Eastbourne

A CIP Record for this book is
available from the British Library

ISBN-10 0 7486 1469 9 (hardback)
ISBN-13 9 7807 4861 469 1 (hardback)
ISBN-10 0 7486 1470 2 (paperback)
ISBN-13 9 7807 4861 470 7 (paperback)

The right of Nigel Dower to be identified
as author of this work has been asserted in
accordance with the Copyright, Designs and
Patents Act 1988.

CONTENTS

PREFACE

Shortly before writing these words, I turned on Google – my favourite search engine on the Web – and typed in phrases like 'world citizens', 'global citizenship' and 'global citizen' and discovered that, for instance, for 'world citizens' there were 2,200,000 search results and for 'global citizens' 1,070,000! Some refer to organisations, some to texts; many of the search results refer to the same organisations and texts. Nevertheless, such figures are striking. They illustrate at least three things. First, there is great interest in the ideas of global citizenship or world citizenship – ideas I treat as interchangeable. Second, this interest is characteristically premised on the belief that agents have global responsibilities to help make a better world and that they are part of large-scale networks of concern. Global citizenship involves both an ethical component and an institutional component. Third, this interest reflects the fact that many people describe themselves as world citizens or global citizens. This fact does not establish that we are global citizens or that the idea of global citizenship is coherent, since it is possible to believe in what is false or confused. Still, there is a large social phenomenon of hundred of thousands of people acting in the belief that they are global citizens. This at least needs to be explained and understood, even for those who are sceptical about the idea – which I am not.

The specific origins of this book lie in work I have been doing on global citizenship and related issues over the last five years. From 1997 to 1999, I directed a Project on global citizenship at the University of Aberdeen, funded by the Gordon Cook Foundation. In this Project we looked at ways courses in global citizenship might be promoted at university level. This resulted *inter alia*, apart from the Project Report, in *Global Citizenship: A Critical Reader* (Dower and Williams 2002) published by EUP and a contract with

EUP for me to write this book. This book, unlike *World Ethics – the New Agenda* (Dower 1998), which I wrote in 1997 for upper level undergraduate use, is an introductory text book at level one for students in a variety of courses on such topics as politics, international relations, globalisation, global issues, ethics, sociology, citizenship, human rights, environment, peace and development. Whilst it will be apparent that it is written by someone with a background in philosophy, it is intended to be a transdisciplinary text. Its task is to describe, analyse and evaluate an important emerging phenomenon – global citizenship. Whilst it will also be apparent that I favour the idea of global citizenship and develop my own favoured conception of it, my primary purpose is to provide the reader with the tools with which to engage critically with the idea. Apart from its primary target group – level one undergraduates – it is written in the hope that the general reader interested in world affairs finds it enlightening, that members of the international NGO community and those in government and inter-government agencies are helped to reflect critically on what they do, and that it appeals to those in sixth-year studies in schools.

My interest in global citizenship goes back a long way. I had really absorbed the 'global point of view' from my parents' example, precepts and interests. A year teaching as a Quaker VSO in Kenya in 1964–5 opened up my horizons but it was not until the early 1970s that I got involved in the NGO scene, particularly the local branches of the World Development Movement and of the United Nations Association. These interests continued, after a three-year period teaching at the University of Zimbabwe (1983–6), in other bodies as well, like Quaker Peace & Service and the International Development Ethics Association. I do not recall when it was that I first started calling myself a world or global citizen. Certainly by the mid-1980s, when I has started teaching courses on the ethics of international relations, I was advancing cosmopolitanism and applying it as a critique of states and as a basis of action by individuals. But until about 1997 I had taken cosmopolitanism and global/world citizenship to be at bottom the commitment to a global ethic or ethic of global responsibility. Whilst that remains a key element in the idea, and for many people is really what their commitment to being a global citizen is all about, I have realised in the last five years that the idea is lot more complicated and controversial than that. This book is the record of that realisation.

A sympathetic interest in global citizenship – whatever its complexities – is unlikely unless someone does indeed have some kind of personal commitment to a global ethic. Where does that commitment come from? Apart from a general sketching of different approaches to global ethics, I do not go into the grounding of a global ethic in any depth. This is partly because this book is not meant to be primarily about the philosophical basis of global ethics: it is definitely not a repetition, even a partial repetition, of ideas and arguments in *World Ethics – the New Agenda* (Dower 1998), to which the reader is referred if she wants my more extended philosophical discussion of these issues. It is also partly because I stress that commitment to common or shared values and norms may come from many different sources – philosophies, theologies or worldviews. It so happens that the grounding of my own global ethic is a blend of philosophical views about the nature of human well-being and a Quaker belief that there is 'that of God' in everyone and that we all called to 'answer' that of God in everyone. But I assume that there are many, many ways of understanding one's global ethic – both religious and secular – sufficient to support shared values in the world and one's wish to realise them. My Quakerism, now stated, remains my background – it is not the public foreground of the book. The minimalism of this statement, some might say its understatement, is actually one of the statements of the book.

Whilst I locate the discussion in the context of the wider literature generally (though not as much as I would have liked), I make particular references to the Reader referred to above – the first I believe on this topic – that John Williams and I edited. This book can be seen as a companion to that Reader, not because it tracks the discussions – it does not do this at all – but because it complements and expands the underlying framework for many of the more detailed discussions of the range of global issues the Reader's writers deal with. For instance, if you are particularly interested in following up on specific global issues such as the impact of technology, immigration, economic globalisation, the United Nations and European citizenship, the chapters by Strybos, Ottonelli, Newlands, Imber and Føllesdal deal fully with these respectively. If the development of specific approaches to global ethics is wanted, the chapters by Küng, Alkire and van den Anker serve well, as do Attfield's and Smyth and Blackmore's pieces on environmental issues, and Hutchings, on a feminist approach. The critical issues concerning global citizenship's relation to globalisation, international relations and global democracy are usefully explored by Falk, Williams, Held, Miller and Axtmann.

A book on this topic can hardly fail to make reference to the tragic events of 11 September 2001 and their aftermath. I have placed my main discussion of this at the end of the book. This is both because I do not see those events reducing the relevance or affecting the character of global citizenship and because my responses to them are partly informed by what I say about global citizenship.

My thanks are due to many people but in particular to members of the Project and those who attended its closing conference for generally stimulating my thinking; to the students in the first four years of a 'global citizenship' course for their comments on and responses to materials I have tried out on them; and to those who read and commented on the draft version of all or parts of this book: Liz Ashford, Martin Bayliss, Nicola Carr, Ian Davidson, Gayle Dower, Mary Dower, Ernie Dunster, Ralph Dutch, Eileen Grant, Josh

Hursey, Annalisa Maccio, Julia Nevarez, Michael Partridge, Brian Phillips, John Smith, Martin Weber and John Williams. I am also grateful to Derek Heater for allowing me to see and use the pre-publication text of his latest book (Heater 2002).

This book is dedicated to my mother Jean Dower, whose interest and encouragement have always been an inspiration to me.

Nigel Dower
May 2002

GLOSSARY

The purpose of this Glossary is not to provide dictionary definitions but brief accounts of what some key words and phrases refer to.

Citizenship: membership, determined by factors such as place of birth, parentage or naturalisation, of a political community (generally a nation-state), in virtue of which one has legally defined rights and duties, significant identity and (on some accounts) moral responsibility to participate in public affairs.

Communitarianism: a social/political philosophy according to which moral, social and political values are constituted by the social relations within an established society or community with a shared tradition. Some communitarians question whether global society/community exists, whilst others assert its existence in embryonic form.

Cosmopolitanism: an ethical theory according to which all human beings belong to one domain and in principle have obligations towards one another across that domain. Although some still note the etymological meaning of 'cosmopolitan' as 'citizen (polites) of the universe/world (cosmos)', it is generally taken to be a robust form of a global ethic. It provides a critical framework for assessing the foreign policy of states and is in contrast to internationalism and sceptical realism.

Environmentalism: active engagement in protecting the environment. Two kinds of approach underlie it. Anthropocentrism: the natural world and non-human life do not have intrinsic value independent of us and are there for human beings to use sustainably. Biocentrism: the natural world or the environment is not simply there for humans to use, non-human life has an intrinsic value independent of human interests and therefore humans ought to respect nature.

Ethic: a set of norms (duties/rights) and values (good/virtues) answering the question 'how ought one to act?' that guides the decisions of an individual or social group whose ethic it is. It can also include, lying behind them, an ethical theory, story or worldview that both justifies these norms and values and gives meaning to them. A global ethic either refers to the universal norms and values accepted by an individual or group, or it refers to norms and values that are shared by people throughout the world and expressed in public practices, declarations and so on.

Ethics: sustained, critical and systematic reflection on the nature and justification of an ethic or morality. Such reflection, generally conducted by philosophers and other academic theorists, takes further the more informal reflections anyone can have about their moral values and principles. Global ethics is enquiry into the nature and justification of ethical norms as they apply globally and into issues that are global in character.

Global civil society: civil society is the matrix of social relationships and organisations in a society – other than political institutions and economic institutions (schools, churches, charities, neighbourhood groups) – through which shared or public goods are pursued. At the global level, NGOs and communications networks (for example, through the Internet) constitute examples of global civil society.

Global democracy: international arrangements whereby individuals can act democratically to influence decisions made outside their nation-state about global affairs that significantly affect them. Cosmopolitan democracy is a formalised version.

Global governance: the patterns of decision-making and the institutions that facilitate them whereby human beings order their public affairs at a global level or co-operate in respect to common global problems. Governance is distinct from government, which is reliant on regulation by coercion and is the most conspicuous form of governance. There are many forms of global governance.

Globalisation: the economic, political and cultural process whereby individuals and corporate bodies increasingly perform actions that have impacts across/throughout the world and perceive themselves, through the deterritorialisation of social space, as having global identities, concerns and impacts. The process has been going on over centuries but it was only in the 1990s that the phenomenon of globalisation came to dominate public consciousness.

Human rights: rights held by all human beings in virtue of their common humanity. They may be thought of as fundamental moral rights or as legal rights established by international law – either way they are contrasted with legal and moral rights, which exist in virtue of the legal system or conventions of a particular society. If global citizenship is in part constituted by the possession of rights, the rights in question are human rights.

Internationalism: the claim in international relations that there is an international society or society of nation-states, which as a society is governed by moral norms such as respect for sovereignty and rules against aggression. Such a conception of international relations is contrasted to both realism and cosmopolitanism. If states can be viewed as citizens of the society of states, then international citizenship may be seen as one form of global citizenship.

Kantianism: the ethical approach, based on the philosophy of Immanuel Kant, that founds (cosmopolitan) morality on respect for all human beings as people; respect for persons is based on the fact that human beings are rational agents. Kantianism is based on the principle of universalisability: 'so act that you will the maxim of your action to be universal law'.

Libertarianism: a social and political philosophy according to which the basic value morality should defend is liberty: individuals should allow one another as much liberty as possible and the state should not interfere in people's lives beyond what is minimally necessary to maintain liberty and public order. An important dimension of liberty is economic liberty. Thus libertarianism underpins the free market, including the global free market.

NGO: a non-governmental organisation, such as one made up of individuals working for a global goal, such as combating poverty, saving the whale or resisting the death penalty, and supported largely by voluntary contributions of money and time from other individuals. International NGOs are called INGOs. Active global citizenship finds much of its practical expression through NGOs.

Patriotism: an attitude of loyalty on the part of a citizen towards her own country. Since global citizenship can be seen as an attitude of loyalty towards all of humanity, these two attitudes may seem to be in conflict and sometimes are. A global citizen need not be unpatriotic, though her patriotism will have to be a *critical* patriotism.

Peace: the absence of war or violent conflict in the relations of individuals and groups with one another. A community that fully enjoys peace has to have this relationship with all the groups it interacts with at the time and into the foreseeable future. Peace is an important value because it is the prerequisite for the meaningful performance of most other human activities. Peace can also be defined less negatively as the presence of harmonious relationships (shalom).

Realism: a theory of international relations contrasted to cosmopolitanism and internationalism that stresses the difficult and dangerous nature of politics amongst sovereign states. Realists are thus often sceptical about the possibility and/or the applicability of ethical principles, arguing that the need for power and security overrides such restraints or limitations on policy. Realism stresses states as by far the most significant actors in shaping the world in which we live, seeing individuals, NGOs, corporations and international organisations as playing a far less important part.

Relativism: the view that moral values vary from culture to culture. As a robust thesis, it challenges the thesis of global ethics that there are universal values or that there is one global domain of moral values (and hence challenges the normal ethical assumption lying behind global citizenship); as a weaker thesis, it serves as a reminder that a global ethic must recognise the legitimate variations in the values of different societies.

Responsibility: the ethical norm, generally accepted and advocated by global citizens, according to which individuals have duties to further human well-being and combat what impedes it, such as injustices; these duties go beyond the duties of morality in ordinary day-to-day interactions.

Rights: a claim that can be made by or on behalf of a person to some benefit such as liberty, privacy, security, food or medical care, that agents – either specific agents or agents in general – have corresponding duties to respect, protect, promote or provide. A right may be a moral right (in virtue of a moral practice or theory) or a legal right (in virtue of a legal system, national or international).

United Nations: the international organisation set up in 1945 after World War II with the primary objective of providing international security but with other objectives such as economic advancement for all countries and the protection of human rights. All countries are members of the United Nations (currently about 190).

Universalism: the ethical idea that there are universal values and norms which either *are* accepted or *ought to be* accepted by people in all parts of the world.

Universalism is often regarded with suspicion, either by relativists or by those who regard what is presented as universal values as really being a projection of Western or Enlightenment values onto the rest of the world. However, most ethical theories – and certainly those that can be seen as global ethics – do have some universal elements, for instance the universal norm of respecting diversity and universal value of freedom from starvation.

Utilitarianism: the ethical theory that says an action is right if it promotes the best balance of good over evil. Classically, this was seen by Mill and Bentham as the greatest happiness principle but more recent Utilitarians prefer to talk about maximising interests or the satisfaction of preferences.

Value: that which is regarded as good or desirable by an agent. Values may be non-moral, such as those things that constitute an individual human being's flourishing or well-being, or they may be moral, such as the virtue of honesty or the duty not to steal. Sometimes values are contrasted with norms, where values refer to what is good (morally and non-morally) and norms refer to principles guiding choice, such as moral, legal, political rules, duties or obligations (as in the phrase 'norms and values' in this book) but in other contexts values embrace moral norms as well.

World government: a form of political rule (sometimes referred to as world federalism) in which the whole world would be under the government of one central authority and nation-states would no longer exist as separate sovereign states but rather, if at all, as regional governments. Advocates hope that it would be democratic, critics fear it would be global tyranny.

World poverty: a condition of absolute poverty characterised by malnutrition, hunger, extensive disease, disempowerment and short life-expectancy, experienced by over a billion of the world population (one sixth), mainly in the so-called developing countries of the world. Tackling it is a primary object of global responsibility for both governments and individuals.

PART I

THE FRAMEWORK

1. INTRODUCTION

SOURCES OF INTEREST

Why is there an interest in the idea of global citizenship, especially in the last thirty years? There are four main factors: the increasing pressure of global problems requiring common solutions; the general phenomenon of globalisation; revived interest in the idea of citizenship itself; and a revived interest in the perennial approach of cosmopolitanism, often called nowadays 'global ethics'.

These factors are interconnected but it is useful to present them initially as separate factors. They are indicated briefly here but are the subject matter of later chapters. Indeed, the chapter as a whole is intended both to give the reader an overview of the general direction and content of the book and at the same time to act as a flyer for many ideas that are mentioned here and developed later on.

Global problems

Environmental problems provide the most obvious and frequently invoked global problems eliciting global citizenship responses. Indeed, the Review of the UK Toyne Report (Toyne 1993), which had argued the case for more environmental education at university level in the UK, explicitly linked such courses on environmental responsibility to global citizenship (Khan 1996). It is not hard to see why. Many environmental problems, such as global warming, are global because their impacts are caused by actors all over the world and because the solutions depend on co-ordinated action by all or most countries. This is particularly pertinent for global citizenship because there are many things that individuals can do to help preserve the environment and thus contribute to exercising global responsibility.

There are many other kinds of global problems which require co-ordinated responses: world poverty and lack of development in many poor countries; the trafficking in drugs; AIDS; human rights violations in many countries and so on. Perhaps of greater significance are the problems of global peace and security and what needs to be done in a world wracked by countless wars, and now, since 11 September 2001, even more concerned with the challenge of global terrorism.

Globalisation

Globalisation has also played a crucial role in creating the social and intellectual environment in which ideas of global citizenship have flourished. It is common to think of globalisation as the development of global capitalism but, as we shall see, this is a seriously one-sided view of the phenomenon. Following Scholte, I shall identify at least four dimensions to it: production, community, governance and knowledge. Each of them illustrates how social relations have become global in the sense of becoming deterritorialised, in other words de-linked from a particular territory such as one's nation-state (Scholte 2000). When I first used the Web search engine Google a few years ago, it claimed to search over 1.5 *billion* sites in about one and a half seconds (it is now over 2 billion). I remember having one of those moments of realisation: this was what globalisation was all about. It was not just the fact that information about the world was there at the press of a key; it was the sense that I was *connected* to all these sites. The sense of a 'global village' or a 'global neighbourhood' – a phrase promoted by a recent influential Report of the Commission on Global Governance (CGG 1995) – now has a great amount of psychological reality.

Anyway, as an aspect of the complex process of globalisation new patterns of human interactions and relations have emerged – in particular, various forms of 'global governance' and new forms of association in 'global civil society', notably through non-governmental organisations (NGOs). As many individuals acting outside formal government play active roles, usually through organisations or through informal networking, it is natural for many to see themselves as acting as 'citizens' in this new global polity in which the nation-state is no longer the only key player in global affairs. The rise of interest in global citizenship is an aspect of globalisation.

Citizenship

Running parallel to this, but with at least partially different sources of interest, has been increased attention, especially in the last fifteen years, paid to the idea of citizenship itself. Citizenship has become a highly contested concept amongst theorists offering different conceptions of it. This is partly because of a revival of interest in citizenship as an active civic virtue in the face of increasing apathy amongst voters whose primary interests are focused more on private consuming than on active participation in public affairs. But this debate, sometimes seen as the liberal/republican debate, intersects with another debate about citizenship in a multi-ethnic society concerning the proper representation of minority group interests, which are not properly recognised let alone protected in traditional understandings of liberal democracy. Thus, there is much uncertainty about what is really 'central' to the concept.

In so far as citizenship is linked to democracy, another challenge is the problem of the 'democratic deficit', the increasing realisation that citizens cannot really exercise control over their shared destiny because so much of what happens to a country is determined not by national politics but by forces outside it. These forces are the greater roles of international and regional institutions (like the EU for European countries) or the greater influence of non-governmental economic actors like transnational companies. So there is at least interest in the idea of 'citizenship in a globalised world'. One natural way of understanding this phrase is in terms of an extension of the idea of citizenship to global citizenship, although one does not have to take that route or accept that extension. Thus, interest in global citizenship partly 'piggybacks' on the back of an interest in citizenship itself.

Cosmopolitanism

The fourth factor to be mentioned here is the perennial appeal of cosmopolitanism itself. The idea of being a 'cosmo-polities' – literally a 'citizen of the universe' – goes back to the ancient Graeco-Roman world, particularly to the thought of the Stoics. Stoicism was a religious/philosophical movement in which people practised and advocated a life of virtue in accordance with reason, and which had a major influence in the ancient world from roughly the third century BC to the second century AD, until Christianity displaced it. For the Stoics, human beings were members or 'citizens' of a more fundamental community than that of their particular city, state or empire of which they might be politically citizens: the latter citizenship was an accident of birth and circumstance. There was a universal or global moral order – universal values and duties in one's relations to any member of this larger moral community. Whilst the specific idea of global *citizenship* popular with the Stoics was later not generally accepted for a long time – it reappeared in the Enlightenment, receded again in the nineteenth century, only to gain acceptance by some again in the twentieth century – the basic idea of a *universal ethic* binding all human beings together in one moral community has been a fairly standard feature of thinking both in the Western tradition and in other traditions.

In the twentieth century, particularly in the second half, globalisation produced greater knowledge about the world and greater capacity to act at a distance. This involved an increasing realisation that this universal ethic, which had always in principle linked people to one another throughout the world, now had numerous and significant *applications*. There were now things involving global relations of various kinds that ordinary people (as opposed to government representatives) both could do and should do. Thus, particularly from the 1970s onward, the duty to give aid to help alleviate extreme poverty in other parts of the world became for many an actual and pressing application of a universal ethic. Cosmopolitanism came to be seen not merely as a utopian ideal of a few but as a more realistic guide for individual action for many, and also as the basis for a critique of what states do in relation to one another. Thus, global problems and the forces of globalisation have created a context for global ethics to have a real role in decision-making, and in so far as one strand of citizenship is the idea of responsibility, this interest in global ethics feeds into the interest in global citizenship. (It should be added that not all advocates of global citizenship or global ethics necessarily see this underlying ethic as a timeless ethic that has always been accepted.)

THE IDEA OF GLOBAL CITIZENSHIP

If someone claims that she is a global citizen, she is making a claim (1) about the status of all human beings and (2) a claim about herself as someone who accepts the status of being a global citizen.

1. The basic status of being global citizens has three components: a

normative claim about how humans should act, an existential claim about what is the case in the world and an aspirational claim about the future. (The term 'existential' has no link with 'existentialism'; for most readers 'factual' or 'empirical' might be easier but these terms rule out possible 'metaphysical' or religiously inspired interpretations like the kingdom of heaven.)

The normative claim is that, as global citizens, we have certain duties that in principle extend to all human beings anywhere in the world and that all human beings have a certain moral status of being worthy of moral respect.

The existential claim is that, in being citizens of the world, we are members of some kind of global community, usually but not always understood as institutional or quasi-political in character.

The aspirational claim builds on the normative and existential claim in stating that the world can and should become one in which basic values are realised more fully and this requires the strengthening of such factors as community, institutions, legal framework and so on.

2. Implications of this for someone who accepts the status: a self-conscious global citizen accepts *in varying degrees* certain kinds of engagement as an 'active' global citizen in exercising responsibility or asserting universal rights, and certain attitudes towards human beings in general.

This description of the basic idea is both ambitious and vague at the same time. It is ambitious in that my thesis is that in almost all cases (to say 'all' would be unwise given the fluidity of the concept) a person's conception of global citizenship contains all three elements, albeit with different emphases on the different elements. It is vague in that it allows for a very wide range of interpretations of each of the three elements and the kinds of active engagement accepted.

My picture of a typical 'active' global citizen

First, a person has the following global moral perspective: all human beings have certain fundamental rights and all human beings have duties to respect and promote these rights. The world is far from being a place in which these rights are adequately realised. There are many causes of this, not least the self-interested priorities of nation-states in their foreign polices and the harsh effects of economic globalisation pursued on neo-liberal lines. Her ethical perspective provides her with both a basis for criticising what governments and companies do and also a basis for personal commitment actively to pursue an agenda in some chosen area such as poverty alleviation, protecting the environment, working for peace and against the denial of human rights. The degree of active engagement varies considerably. The global citizen need be no more active than a typical person who has some social concerns in her life. That then is the typical normative component and the kind of active engagement it leads to.

A typical global citizen does not act alone nor does she think of herself as an isolated individual. At the least, she sees herself as part of some kind of global community of like-minded people and those whose problems she shares. But generally, she acts with others and through organisations that advance her causes. She may join political parties and to try and influence foreign policies. She may join NGOs and support their work. She may network with like-minded people through, for instance, the Internet. She sees her actions as a citizen as mediated through various forms of association and organisation. 'Citizen' means more than 'agent'; it connotes engagement in some kind of public action that takes place in a public space made up of associations, institutions and networks. This constitutes the 'existential' component through which she can act.

A global citizen is, however, a cautious optimist. She is engaged in what she does because she feels that it is possible that the world could become a better place with less violence, poverty, environmental degradation and violation of human rights. She may not have confidence that it will become so. However, she believes it is worth the endeavour to try and bring about a better world community. In order for this to come about, certain institutions in the world need to be strengthened, reformed and improved – a reformed UN, perhaps, or stronger NGOs with more access to the decision-making of international bodies. This then is the aspirational component she accepts and may choose to promote.

The primacy of the normative?

For many people who think of themselves as global citizens, the normative element is the most important. To say that she is a global citizen is to say that she accepts some kind of global ethic and that she ought to do her bit in her preferred way to promote these values. If this were all that were involved in claims about global citizenship, namely the assertion of responsibility based on a global ethic, then the word 'citizen' would carry no specific meaning and all that one would need to discuss would be the 'pros and cons' of a global ethic or one's preferred version of it. The discussion of this book is premised on the view that there is much more involved in the idea of global citizenship, as revealed in the second and third elements.

However, even the view that global citizenship is really a normative claim does contain (albeit implicitly) some reference to the second and third elements, since some kind of real moral community within which one is acting is usually assumed, as is a modest optimism that the world both can and should be made a better place by strengthening the moral community of the world. And it is precisely the thinness of these specifications of the second and third elements that leaves both the more ambitious advocate of global citizenship and the typical critic of global citizenship dissatisfied. A more robust conception of global citizenship in terms of the institutional and aspirational claims is what is needed and is defended in what follows.

We have already identified one significant area of disagreement about global citizenship: that between a primarily ethical conception (without much else) and a more robust account. Let us now identify several of the major areas of contention over what turns out to be a surprisingly controversial concept! Here are some of the various issues that are discussed more fully later on, especially in Part III.

SOME ISSUES

Are we global citizens?

There are issues that turn on the question whether or not we are global citizens. Here we distinguish four challenges. First, that there is no global ethic: we really should not accept a global ethic, since ethics is relative to culture. If we do not accept a global ethic, the whole ethical core of global citizenship is undermined. Second, that there are no relevant institutions: the relevant institutions at the global level needed to make us global citizens simply do not exist. We certainly do not have world government (which some critics will insist is what is needed) nor do we have sufficiently robust global institutions to constitute the 'citizen' element. Neither the United Nations nor the networks making up global civil society (a much disputed phenomenon itself anyway) provide the right kind of basis for global citizenship. Third, that the idea is redundant: the idea of global citizenship is in fact redundant or vacuous because we can make all the global ethical claims we want about global responsibilities and rights without invoking the idea! Fourth, that we do not need any reform: the implicit aspirational element in global citizenship is misguided, since the world, whatever its faults, is structurally and institutionally sound and what we need is a better functioning international order of states, not new-fangled forms of governance or the interference by individuals in global affairs!

There are also interpretational issues. We saw above that there is an issue between a primarily ethical conception and a more robust one including the existential and aspirational elements. Assuming here the more robust idea, the reader should be aware that, amongst other issues, the following are significant.

What kind of global ethic?

Given that there is some kind of global ethic embedded in global citizenship, what kind of ethic are we talking about? Let us suppose that a global ethic specifies universal values (life, subsistence, security, liberty, pleasure, rationality) and norms (do not kill, steal, lie) and global responsibilities (duties we have in principle towards one another across the globe). This, however, leaves a lot of issues unresolved.

We can ask: is this global ethic something a global citizen believes is as a matter of fact universally accepted everywhere or rather, since 'universally' is rather strong, at least *generally* accepted in all or nearly all cultures and societies throughout the world? Or is it rather a set of values and norms a global citizen accepts and advocates as *applicable* to all people in the world, even though she knows full well that they are not generally accepted and acted on? If the global ethic accepted is of the latter kind, a further question arises: is it an ethical view held by a global citizen because she believes it to be timelessly true, objectively valid or rationally required? Or does she simply see her global ethic as based on personal preference, albeit a preference based on careful reflection on how she wants not only herself but people around her or in the world as a whole to act and organise themselves socially? Furthermore, how relevant is the emergence of 'global community' to the justification of global citizenship? Perhaps the relevant global ethic is neither to be thought of as a pre-existing universal consensus, nor something that is asserted by the individual thinker, but as something that is emerging in the world through negotiation, dialogue and consensus-building – as a result of the need for people in the late twentieth and early twenty-first centuries to forge a basis for getting on in a fragile planet.

The theory and content of a global ethic?

Linked to the questions about the form the global ethic takes, there are more straightforward questions about the interpretation of and the substance of our preferred global ethic. What theories or worldviews support the norms and values of a global ethic? Religious worldviews like Christianity or Buddhism? Philosophical views like natural law, human rights or Utilitarianism (to be explained later)? How important are these theories as opposed to the values and norms they support? I shall argue that a global citizen has very little reason to be hostile to other global citizens whose theories or worldviews are different, so long as there is general convergence on the values and norms to be promoted and followed in the world. This is one aspect of respect for diversity.

On the other hand, there may also be differences in the norms and values themselves that different global citizens will advocate both as goals and means. Thus, an economic libertarian may advocate a largely unregulated free market as the main value for the world but a social democrat may reject such a core value as *the* global value and advocate social justice. A protester against Trident submarines may be willing to break the law but other peace activists may be unwilling to break the law. They may all, however, be global citizens.

All or some?

A rather different issue is this: are we all global citizens or only some of us global citizens? It may be said that we all have a certain status as moral beings, with certain rights and responsibilities, and this is true of us even if we do not acknowledge it. As Piet Hein once said, 'we are global citizens with tribal souls': objectively we make global impacts and have global responsibilities but we do not have the appropriate consciousness through which we generally recognise it – though some of us do some of the time (quoted in Barnaby 1988: 192). It seems odd, however, to say someone is a global citizen if she does nothing to promote a better world or does not claim her rights and so on. Global citizenship seems to involve active engagement of some kind and some kind of self-identification as a global citizen. It is only in this sense that one can advocate global citizenship, since if we all are anyway, then there is nothing to advocate.

I develop an account of global citizenship that makes sense of both intuitions. Global citizenship at one level is indeed about a universal status and about a certain kind of global reality in which anyone can become involved; but in a fuller sense, parallel to the idea of citizenship as active engagement within a state, only some do take on the active role. There is an analogy here with the remark of John Locke, the seventeenth-century political philosopher, that we 'are born free and rational' (Locke 1960: ch. 5). Of course, he knew that a baby had not developed his powers of rationality and moral freedom, which require education and appropriate conditions; rather it was an assertion of a certain status and a certain potentiality.

What kind of institutional embodiment?

Finally, we can ask: granted global citizenship involves some institutional embodiment (either as something existing or as something to be worked for), just what is that embodiment? Are informal global social networks sufficient? Do we need the existence of a matrix of institutional associations like NGOs or political parties through which agents can act? Do global economic corporations provide a significant aspect of global citizenship (called corporate global citizenship)? Does the UN provide the right framework? Do we need something new like global democracy? Or do we need to think in terms of world government?

Linklater sets out the challenge thus in a useful survey chapter on global citizenship, 'What [does] cosmopolitanism mean in a world in which there may be global governance but there is no global government to define the rights and duties of world citizens?', and suggest three key aspects: 'cosmopolitan duties alongside duties to the state', rights based on 'cosmopolitan law' and 'the political project of and strengthening process of creating a world-wide public sphere alongside the public spheres that exist separately within democratic states' (Linklater 2002).

My conception

The primary purpose of the book is to set out the analytic and empirical framework for thinking carefully and critically about global citizenship but there does underlie it a certain conception. By 'conception' (following Rawls 1971: 10) I mean a particular interpretation and elaboration of the more basic 'idea' or 'concept' of global citizenship as indicated earlier. A particular conception is, of course, something some other thinkers reject but in rejecting it they are not rejecting the general idea – for which they may have their own preferred conception.

I develop my conception both because I think it is the most fruitful way of thinking about global citizenship and because, given this interpretation, it is applicable to the world now and so we are now global citizens. My conception emerges as we proceed because it rationalises why I focus on certain things, for example on human rights (because for me, but not for all, bearing human rights is an aspect of global citizenship), on NGOs (because for me acting through NGOs is engagement in global citizenship institutions) and on governance (because for me it makes sense to say that we are even now participating democratically in global governance).

WHY IS GLOBAL CITIZENSHIP IMPORTANT AS AN AREA OF ACADEMIC ENQUIRY?

First, it is an idea whose time has come. The idea has come to be incorporated into the thinking and engaged actions of an increasingly large number of people whose sense of global responsibility and identity is expressed through their own self-descriptions as global citizens and who act through various kinds of institutions, associations and networks seen by many as the public embodiment of this idea. At least there is a large social phenomenon that needs to be investigated and understood, including the fact that many others are sceptical of the claims of global citizenship. Understanding why such an idea is so contested is itself a matter of academic interest. Recent books on the subject attest to a recent surge of academic interest (for example, Carter 2001; Cohen 1996; Heater 1996, 2002; Hutchings and Dannreuther 1999).

Second, an enquiry like this is important because what it is about is important. Such an enquiry is likely to make people more informed about and sympathetic to the idea. At least my enquiry is intended to have these effects. An academic enquiry need not make someone sympathetic to what one is enquiring about, even if the author intended it – someone reading this book might come away less sympathetic than when she started! Nevertheless, if the second reason is sound, it presupposes the importance of people taking on the idea of global citizenship and it may be asked: why is that important? Its importance will, I hope, become clear as the book proceeds but two thoughts may be added here.

At one level we are, if my thesis is correct, global citizens anyway, whether we realise it or not. So it might be asked: if that is so, why does it matter that people come to accept it? Apart from an age-old presumption that it is better to know what is true about oneself than be ignorant of it, it matters greatly in practical terms because an acceptance of one's status will make one understand responsibilities and rights in a certain way, and thus make it more likely that one will act. Active global citizenship does make a difference because states, individually and collectively, are unable to protect the common good adequately and there is a large role for individuals acting in civil society, globally as well as nationally.

Nevertheless, from the outset it must be accepted that effective global agency does not depend upon accepting global citizenship or being interested in the idea of it. Nothing in this account is intended to discredit or render inappropriate the kind of commitment that many people have to make the world a better place by their efforts *without using the language of global citizenship*. A strong-willed person with clear moral convictions may act in isolation or through groups and organisations like a church, and have other forms of self-identity. The discourse of global citizenship is merely one way, though I wish to suggest a powerful way, in which many individuals choose to identify themselves and by so doing become energised and committed to the actions they take. On the view I am taking, there are many such active engaged people working for a better world who are implicitly active global citizens.

The Plan of the Book

Part I: The framework

Part I sets out the framework for thinking about global citizenship. This chapter, which indicates the general approach and main elements, serves as a minimal basis for the other chapters in that any of the latter can be usefully read without the reader having read the ones in between.

In Chapter 2 'Global Perspective and Problems: The Need for a Global Ethic' we look at a global or cosmopolitan ethic as the basic ethical orientation of global citizenship. This requires us to look at the history and development of global ethical theories, and at the kinds of global problems confronting us at the beginning of the twenty-first century and thus necessitating a global response in which there is an important role for individuals.

Chapter 3 'Citizenship in a Globalised World' looks at the idea of citizenship in a globalised context. Whilst global citizenship has piggybacked on the idea of citizenship, at the same time it can be seen as embedded in various processes of globalisation, especially in emerging forms of global civil society and global governance.

Part II: Examples and areas of interest

This Part focuses on four specific areas – human rights, peace and security, world poverty and the environment, and the United Nations and global governance. The aim in these chapters is to outline a particular area of global concern for global citizens, to give some examples of global citizenship in action and to illustrate the range of possible activities. The first chapter is really a bridge between Part I and Part II, since, whilst dealing with an area of concern, it also highlights the rights dimension of global citizenship itself. The fourth chapter of Part II is also a bridge to Part III, since the issues of governance cannot be discussed properly without addressing the normative claims and counter-claims involved – the focus of Part III. In each of these chapters, examples of organisations are given. It may appear invidious to select any for comment, in case they are being seen as singled out for importance. If we remember, however, that 'it is calculated that there are well over 15,000 recognisable NGOs that operate in three of more countries and draw their finances in more than one country' (Axtmann 2002: 103), even listing a proportion of these would only serve to stress the sheer extent of their global presence, without bringing out salient points for our theme. So what is selected is merely chosen to illustrate different aspects of relevance to global citizenship.

In Chapter 4 'Human Rights' we look more closely at the idea of global rights, or what are more usually called human rights. Human rights can both be seen as an ethical theory and as a dimension of international law with a bearing on global citizenship, parallel to the bearing of rights for ordinary citizenship. The UN *Universal Declaration of Human Rights* illustrates the development of international law, and Amnesty International, Human Rights Watch and the International Criminal Court all illustrate aspects of global citizenship.

In Chapter 5 'Peace and Security' the central value of peace is explored and its relationship with security outlined. Aspects of typical global citizenship are shown in certain conceptions of international relations and world order that are non-militaristic and non-nationalistic, and certain attitudes toward cultural, religious and ethnic diversity. Several examples of global citizenship action are given as illustrations: the peace movement, the World Court Project and Trident Ploughshares. These examples also illustrate an important point: global citizens may differ profoundly on the tactics they wish to adopt, particularly in the area of civil disobedience.

Chapter 6 'Development and the Environment' first surveys some of the ethical arguments for being concerned about these matters and also the need to think of them together, for example through the idea of sustainable development or the values of the Earth Charter. Various examples of citizen action are considered, such as working through the World Development Movement, Médecins Sans Frontières and Jubilee 2000, and Oxfam's Global Citizenship programme is introduced.

In Chapter 7 'The United Nations and Global Governance' we look more at global political structures, both as they are now and as they might be reformed. The United Nations is clearly of central importance to such an enquiry – whether one is for it or against it. Should global citizens support the UN? Granted the UN needs reforming, in what ways should it be reformed? Quite apart from that, there are other forms of global governance we need to consider, such as cosmopolitan democracy, and not least the idea of world government. What are the arguments for and against the latter?

Part III: Theoretical issues

In this Part we turn back to more theoretical issues. In most of Parts I and II the broad idea of global citizenship as outlined in the first chapter is accepted, with a promissory note attached: I will deal with the critical issues later. Of course, during earlier discussions a number of critical issues are raised and discussed to some extent. But here we change gear a little. We consider more systematically the critical issues surrounding the idea of global citizenship and defend the general idea plus, where appropriate, my own conception of it in particular. The two chapters divide fairly naturally according to the normative and the other two aspects of the basic idea.

Thus, Chapter 8 'Critique of the Global' considers the idea of a global ethic in more depth and then surveys a wide range of objections such as relativism in ethics, communitarianism in social and political philosophy and realism in international relations, including the argument that the relative weight of patriotic and communitarian values usually has priority over cosmopolitan values.

The second range of objections considered in Chapter 9 'Global Citizenship in the World? – Present Realities and Future Prospects' comes from various forms of challenge to the whole idea of global citizenship and my conception of it. Are, for instance, the facts about global civil society really relevant to global citizenship? This leads to looking forward to the future and examining critically the aspirational element usually embedded in global citizenship claims. What kind of world do we want? Discussion of different visions highlights the presupposition this book has insisted on all along: the real possibility of choice.

So the book ends and thus, by a happy literary device, this chapter ends with a reminder that global citizenship is premised on optimism – not the wild optimism that simply hopes that things in the world will get better but a measured optimism that it can get better by our own actions and efforts.

QUESTIONS

1. Do you think of yourself as a global (or world) citizen? If so, why? If not, why not?
2. Are all us, some of us or none of us global citizens?
3. Why is there now such interest in global citizenship?
4. What issue, idea or point in this chapter, if any, has struck you as (most) important?

A reader will only be able to make a very preliminary attempt to answer these questions, and might like to return to these questions after reading more of the book.

---

2. GLOBAL PERSPECTIVES AND PROBLEMS: THE NEED FOR A GLOBAL ETHIC

SUMMARY OF KEY POINTS COVERED IN THIS CHAPTER

Global problems
  A wide range of problems
  Environmental problems: compliance and mutual interests
  World poverty: why do we respond?
  What make a problem global? A global ethical perspective
Cosmopolitanism
  Six characteristics of Stoic cosmopolitanism
  Later developments
  Stoic/modern: similarities greater than differences
  Ethical/institutional
  Code for individuals/critique of states and international relations
Global ethics: four approaches
  Objectivism: Kant and Utilitarianism
  Subjectivism
  Pre-existing common core
  Modern construction of a global ethic

THE TASK

In this chapter we look at two main sources of interest in global citizenship – global problems and the perennial ideas of cosmopolitanism and global ethics. We identify a number of global problems and examine why they are *global* problems. Responses to such problems are, at bottom, ethical responses.

These ethical responses include the responses of individuals with global ethical concerns often acting as global citizens. What individuals do makes, or at least is believed by global citizens to make, a difference at the global level. This is because of what they do both acting as individuals outside political frame-works (like giving to charity and saving resources) and persuading govern-ments and companies to change their priorities at the international level. If global problems require co-ordinated responses, the will to do this on the part of governments is largely a function of what citizens (including consumers) taking a global perspective want.

Whilst we examine later a number of different sources of global ethics, here we merely need to note that a global ethic – or at least the kind of global ethic appropriate to global citizenship – goes beyond a merely universalist ethics. This kind of global ethic has two components: a set of universal values and norms seen by the person who believes in a global ethic as applying to all human beings and, in addition, a norm of global responsibility according to which agents have responsibilities to promote what is good anywhere in the world (or, as often as not, to oppose what is bad). Responsibilities are, in principle, global in scope. The phrase 'in principle' is important because the extent and mode of action at a distance that any individual can and should engage in may, in practice, be quite limited, given the many other moral factors involved in decision-making. Someone who accepts a global ethic as including this dimension is willing, as occasion arises, to support efforts to alleviate world poverty, to do some recycling for the sake of the environment, go on a peace vigil, write on behalf of Amnesty International and so on. (I do not mean that any person does or should do all of these particular things or indeed any of them – they are merely given as examples of kinds of action.)

GLOBAL PROBLEMS

Here are a number of problems that most people would, without much doubt, regard as global problems: global warming and ozone layer depletion; rapid species loss; soil erosion and desertification; pollution; population growth as a pressure on the environment and a cause of poverty; world poverty, especially hunger and malnutrition and endemic diseases; AIDS; racism and the asso-ciated inequalities that ensue; the status of women in many parts of the world; religious and ethnic hatred; violation of human rights, especially civil rights; economic and sexual exploitation; numerous wars; large-scale movement of refugees; international crime; international terrorism such as the events of September 11th; weapons of mass destruction; proliferation of arms. Most of these items would be accepted as global problems by most thinkers. Some might hesitate about the last two, since they might think that weapons themselves are not the problem but the willingness to use them. Even more might disagree if I added to the list items like the unregulated free market, sovereignty and the overarching pursuit of national interest by states, or the control of patents by rich companies. Such disagreement would not be surprising, since, as I elaborate below, a problem is only a problem relative to a set of values, and people's values differ.

Environmental problems illustrate a particular kind of global problem – those where the problems are caused by agents throughout the world but, more importantly, problems that will not be addressed properly unless co-ordinated action is taken by people and governments throughout the world. This throws up what is known as the compliance problem: how to ensure that, if you or your country make sacrifices or change behaviour that may, for instance, be economically disadvantageous, all or at least most other countries do the same. Otherwise, your efforts or those of a few countries will not make any difference and you will still suffer the environmental problems anyway. It also illustrates another feature of many global problems: that, from the point of view of any country trying to agree on measures to halt or reduce an environmental problem, the reasoning may not appear to be particularly moral if 'moral' here means 'altruistic', since the reason for the co-operation is that without it that country will suffer. This invites the thought that global problems are, at bottom, problems of necessity – that is, what is necessary to protect one's own or one's country's interests. If this is the basis for action, then it hardly looks like an aspect of a global ethic.

But this would be misleading as a general characterisation of global problems. Another major global problem – world poverty – appears to be primarily a problem for poor people, not for rich people. Similarly, if a poor country is poor, it appears to be a problem for the poor country, not for rich countries. So it appears not to be a global problem affecting people everywhere. Of course, we could construe it as a global problem in the above self-interested sense if we say that having a large number of very poor people is bad for the global economy or creates tensions in the world and hence long-term instability. But this really misses the key point: rich people and rich countries are keen, to the extent that they are, to do something about world poverty largely because extreme poverty is an evil they feel *they ought to tackle*. It is a global problem not primarily because it affects our 'non-moral' interests but because, given our moral values, it is something that ought to be alleviated by our collective efforts.

WHAT MAKES A GLOBAL PROBLEM A GLOBAL PROBLEM?

We are now in a better position to see what makes a global problem both a problem and a global one. If we look at the examples listed above, we might at first sight identify three elements that contribute toward making a problem a global one: (a) it is a problem caused by people (or events and processes) from all parts of the world; (b) it is a problem that requires the co-ordinated efforts of many actors from all parts of the world, particularly governments of countries, to solve; (c) it is a problem for significant numbers of people throughout the world. Although all three of these elements apply to most cases, none of them straightforwardly apply to all cases; sometimes problems are caused by a small number of agents from some (not all) parts of the world (consider terrorism); sometimes the solutions depend upon the efforts primarily of some countries (for example, rich countries in tackling world poverty); and, as we have seen, many problems are not problems for all people or countries if we mean by that something that affects those countries or people badly themselves.

But the third element is the most promising if we interpret it morally. What makes a problem a global problem is the fact that some significant evil affects a significant number of people (in many though not necessarily all parts of the world) and there is widespread consensus amongst state actors and individuals interested in world affairs that from a global point of view something ought to be done about this evil. Whether this means that a few governments (for example, rich and powerful ones) should do something, or that governments generally should do so or that in addition many individuals should take up the challenge, is a further question to answer. What makes it a global problem is that something from a global point of view ought to be done by actors outside the country or countries within which the evil exists. Of course, there is usually much to be done by global citizens as contributions toward tackling a global problem. But what makes it global is the global ethical perspective, not who does what. The range of problems we face in the world today are so primarily because, from an ethical point of view, certain evils need to be tackled at a global level: there is in the background some kind of global ethic being appealed to, implicitly or explicitly.

It is because global problems exist that much active global citizenship has emerged as a response. This is because under the conditions of the modern world (partly due to the technologies of global communications and rapid transportation of goods and personnel) individuals have felt empowered to play their part in trying to tackle these problems (Dower 2001). Such problems can no longer be left to the province of governments. Individuals both can and should seek to influence what happens, partly because what governments do is influenced by what individuals do. But increased knowledge about the world and about what happens in other parts of the world will not on its own lead people to do anything about what they know. Nor will increased capacity to do things effectively at a distance on its own lead people to act. Nor indeed will both of these together. What else is needed is motivation. What is needed is commitment to a global ethic, first to the idea that human beings matter anywhere and so whatever evils befall people anywhere are, in principle, of relevance. Commitment is needed too to the idea that one should exercise responsibility to do something – whether a little or a lot – about it oneself.

COSMOPOLITANISM

The question we now need to face is: why is it that global citizens (and indeed other moral agents who do not adopt this self-description) accept a global ethic that includes a commitment to global responsibility? Here we need to look at the history of cosmopolitanism and at various modern approaches to the subject.

Stoic cosmopolitanism

Historically, cosmopolitanism is primarily associated with the ancient Stoics, whose beliefs flourished over about five centuries from the third century BC to the second century AD. It originated in Greece but eventually spread to the whole of the Roman Empire, gradually being displaced later on by Christianity. Its adherents included a number of historical figures still well known today, like Cicero, a Roman statesman and philosopher; Plutarch, a historian; Marcus Aurelius, a Roman emperor; and Epictetus, who was a slave!

The Stoics were not, however, the first thinkers to think of themselves as *cosmo-polites* or 'citizens of the universe'. Diogenes, latterly known as a 'cynic', first adopt the phrase, rejecting Aristotle's claim that 'man is a political animal' – that is, an animal whose nature and essence is realised through membership of particular political community – but claiming that the whole world was his country. He was called a 'cynic' incidentally not because he had what we would now call a cynical view of life – far from it – but rather because he lived very simply like a dog (cyn) in a large tub in the market place. This was intended to shock those around him by challenging the conventions of ordinary city-bound life around him. Socrates, the teacher of Plato in the fifth century BC and another pre-Stoic figure, as reported by Epictetus, also 'took the course when asked of what country he belonged, never to say "I am an Athenian" or "I am a Corinthian" but "I am a citizen of the world" ' (Heater 2002: 29).

The first Stoic so-called was Zeno, who came to Athens to set up his 'school' in 310 BC. (A school was not what we have in mind but rather a centre where men of leisure who wanted to pursue wisdom gathered for discussion under the broad direction of its leader; Plato had earlier formed the famous 'Academy' and, breaking away from him, Aristotle had formed the Lyceum.) He established his school in a distinctive porch (*stoa*) and thus the movement came to be known as Stoicism. There were in fact three waves of Stoicism (often called the early, middle and late Stoas). I do not intend to go into the details of these developments, which belong more to the classical history of philosophy, and instead refer the reader to an excellent and detailed analysis of the historical background by Derek Heater, whose several books in this area have done much to put global citizenship back on the academic agenda and whose ideas I am following here (Heater 1996, 2002). But it is worth noting the long historical development in order to note that Stoicism is not one simple philosophical system but has many variations.

We can, following Heater, identify six main strands of Stoic thought that relate to their conception of cosmopolitanism (though there is much else to Stoicism, of course). These are: the global unity of human beings as one species living in one great world society; the idea of *logos* (speech and rational thought); the idea of universal law; the divine basis of moral law; the role of wisdom; and the goal of harmony.

First and foremost is the root idea of belonging to one world society or community in virtue of our common identity as a species with certain common powers, not least the power of rationality, which includes the capacity for discerning the moral law. As Martha Nussbaum, the classical philosopher who has also done much to advance the global citizenship agenda in recent years, puts it:

> The Stoics, who followed (Diogenes') lead, further developed his image of the *kosmou polites* (world citizen) arguing that each of us dwells, in effect, in two communities – the local community of our birth, and the community of human argument and aspiration that 'is truly great and truly common, in which we look neither to this corner nor to that, but measure the boundaries of our nation by the sun' (Seneca, *De Otio*). It is this community that is, fundamentally, the sources of our moral obligations. With respect to the most basic values, such as justice, 'we should regard all human beings as our fellow citizens and neighbours' (Plutarch, *On the Fortunes of Alexander*). (Nussbaum 1996: 7)

This global community was in some sense a more fundamental community than that of the city-state, nation-state or other political order one happened to belong to. In saying that there are two communities, the emphasis is not on the fact that there are two but rather that there is the wide community of the world or universe and, in contrast to it, other levels of community. In fact, many Stoics recognised that there were several such communities to which a person might belong, such as one's family, one's immediate community, the wide political community. Sometimes the image of concentric circles was evoked. We will later examine critically the implication of these images of concentric circles and multiple loyalties but suffice it to say here that Stoics were reluctant to deny the importance of the obligations one has within more localised communities. Like Socrates, who despite seeing himself as a citizen of the world accepted it as his duty to comply with the decision of his native city's court that he should die by drinking hemlock, many Stoics saw such duties emanating from membership of particular communities as important, as well as one's obligations toward the wider community of all humankind.

What is crucial is the contrast between the accidental nature of one's membership of a particular political community and one's essential nature as a rational human being. In talking, however, of citizenship of a world community they were not talking literally of political community or a wish to create such a worldly community. As Nussbaum noted:

> This clearly did not mean that the Stoics were proposing the abolition of local and national forms of political organisation and the creation of a world state. Their point was even more radical; that we give our first allegiance to no mere form of government, no temporal power, but to the moral community made up by the humanity of all human beings. (Nussbaum 1996: 7)

Although it may be disputed how much of a metaphor the use of the political terminology of citizenship really is, it is clearly a metaphor. It is a rich one, though, since the idea of being a citizen of some kind of a state is supported by two further features: the idea of a universal moral law analogous to the *laws* of a state and the idea of a divine *ruler* as the source of those laws. Whilst the details may be somewhat different, there is this much in common between this Stoic conception and that which Augustine, writing in the sixth century AD, had of the 'earthly city' (made of political communities) and the 'city of God' (made up of all true believers) (Augustine 1947).

To be members of this world community, members have to have the attribute of *logos*, which covers the ideas of speech and reason. These are, of course, linked. The view that rationality was a key characteristic of human beings is not peculiar to the Stoics. It had certainly been widely held by other Greek thinkers such as Aristotle, who famously asserted that human beings could be defined as rational animals. One consequence of this definition was that a divide was assumed to exist between humans and the rest of the animal kingdom (who were not rational) and, whatever the merits or otherwise of Stoic thought, this human-centred or anthropocentric bias has been a source of criticism in more recent times. However, the possession of *logos* or the power of reason was essential if members were to have a crucial feature of membership of a community – the capacity for moral thought and discernment of the rules of morality.

This for the Stoics was understood as being able to understand and follow the 'natural law'. Human beings, no less than the rest of reality, are subject to laws pertaining to their nature such that, if we follow them, then we will realise our nature and achieve our 'good'. This was not, however, a licence to pursue our self-interest but a call to the highest moral virtue and requirements of moral duty. The idea of natural law had a powerful influence on later development in Christianity, especially in the work of the great Catholic theologian of the thirteenth century Thomas Aquinas (Aquinas 1953). The first early statement of it came from a very influential passage in Cicero's *De Re Publica*:

> True law is right reason in agreement with nature; it is of universal application, unchanging and everlasting; it summons to duty by its commands, and averts from wrongdoing by its prohibitions [. . .] we cannot be freed from its obligations by senate or people, and we need not look outside ourselves for an expounder or interpreter of it. (Cicero 1959: III, 22)

This is a forthright example of an approach to ethics that has been influential in our Western tradition and still attractive to many – the idea of an ethic as universal over time and place and in some sense objectively true and discernible by the proper use of our common rational powers.

The conception of moral duty as a kind of law naturally leads to the idea of a lawgiver and this was seen as a divine being (or beings). The idea of the universe being under the direction of a divine being and thus having some meaning and purpose was seen as a basic premise of Stoic cosmopolitanism – but we should not read too much into this, certainly not the rather different conception in Christianity of a personal God.

A common but by no means universal feature of Stoic thought was the idea that real membership of the world community was limited to those who had wisdom. This was linked to the sixth feature, namely the belief that true harmony could be achieved in the world community because it is through wisdom and the cultivation of the moral virtues of moderation and justice that human beings could achieve true harmony in their relations with one another. The Stoics, in many ways, shared the beliefs of Plato and Aristotle earlier – that if only humans could develop their moral powers properly and adopt the right social structures, then the true harmonisation of interests becomes possible.

Subsequent history of cosmopolitanism

Stoic ideas resurfaced again in the Renaissance and Enlightenment, as did more generally the idea of cosmopolitanism. Many Enlightenment thinkers of the eighteenth century thought of themselves as 'citizens of the world', such as Diderot and Voltaire. Part of the Enlightenment approach was to proclaim the universal human power of reason to transcend the limitations of tradition and superstition. Reason, properly used, yielded the same basic truths about the world (as it did most clearly in mathematics) and also the same basic moral principles of human conduct. Those enlightened were largely in Europe and were in the vanguard of a process that would sooner or later sweep the whole world. The idea of human beings belonging to a large single moral community was natural to them. Prominent amongst these thinkers was Immanuel Kant, whose moral thought we look at below. Kant was not a Stoic but his thinking was arguably influenced by that tradition. Cosmopolitan thinking after the eighteenth century rather went into recession, largely because international relations were dominated by concerns amongst theorists about the maintenance of international order through a society of states. The rules that governed this society of states were based on respect for sovereignty and within this model there was very little role for individuals (see Chapter 8).

In the twentieth century, there was increasing interest in cosmopolitan ideas – both in the idea of world citizenship itself and personal global responsibility and also in the idea of a universal ethic as a critical perspective on international relations, though the latter was never particularly dominant compared with internationalism and realism. Mainstream 'internationalism' stressed the rules of a 'morality of states' and, particularly in the period of the Cold War, more 'realist' views of international relations saw international relations as largely an amoral struggle for power and dominance between states. Earlier in the century much of the focus was on working for peace, given the ravages of two world wars. There was much idealism, for instance, in support of the League of Nations, of disarmament conferences and of an idea closely associated with the League's conception, namely the strengthening of international law as the route to international peace (sometimes called 'legal pacifism'). Many people who saw themselves as world citizens supported the idea of world federalism, since world government was seen as the only solution to the problem of war. The focus in cosmopolitan thought in the latter part of the twentieth century broadened to include concerns about absolute poverty, international distributive justice, environmental problems and the increasingly evidenced abuses of human rights throughout the world. Cosmopolitanism also became less linked to the aspiration to create a world government because, for reasons we will look at later, world government came to be seen as neither necessary nor indeed appropriate to the cosmopolitan goals that self-styled global citizens and others adopted.

VARIETIES OF COSMOPOLITANISM

Relevance of Stoic cosmopolitanism

I have focused on the Stoic origins of cosmopolitanism, partly because of its intrinsic interest but partly to illustrate in what respects global citizenship remains the same and in what respects there are or may be significant differences in approaches to global citizenship. Someone might think that what the Stoics had in mind and what I outlined in Chapter 1 as the typical understanding of global citizenship today are so far apart that it might be better to think of them as two different concepts.

The wider community was for the Stoics clearly not a worldly community dependent on political structures, international institutions, actual networks of people linked by NGOs or Internet connections, established international law or accepted declarations of human rights. It was, as the Nussbaum quote above illustrated, an *alternative* to any such contingent human arrangements. This does not make it an imaginary community; it was real enough but at another metaphysical or spiritual level. The contrast might be emphasised by someone who held that global citizenship, as we understand it, is dependent on factors such as globalisation and modern technology. On this view, global citizenship is not a timeless category but is itself contingent on modern conditions.

Although most global citizens would still accept that our membership of a global community is dependent on our being rational agents capable of moral thought, the idea that we are subject to a universal natural law under divine governance would not be accepted by many, since for them global citizenship does not dependent upon religious assumptions, nor would many accept the idea of an objective timeless morality. The conception in terms of a community of the wise may also be seen as elitist and alien to modern conceptions of universal human rights and the idea that we are all global citizens.

In regard to their goal of harmony, we are in the modern era somewhat less optimistic about the human condition, since we are less confident about the real possibility of such social harmony at a deep level. This is because the tendency toward wickedness is seen as more deep-rooted and because the use of reason is not seen as leading so easily to the same conclusions!

This assessment is, however, one-sided. It is true that for many advocating global citizenship in the modern world, the existence and development of 'worldly' institutions and networks are key features – indeed they are for my own conception of global citizenship in the modern world – but the more basic idea of global citizenship allows for all sorts of possibilities. Even for those who focus on the political or institutional dimensions of global citizenship, what underlies this is the idea of a global *moral* community. What makes this a real community (not just an idea in an idealist's head) is either the actual linkages claimed to exist in our modern 'global village' or some deeper metaphysical or religiously conceived community or both.

Of course, the divine basis for a moral order is not something all global citizens would accept but there is nothing in the idea of global citizenship to rule this out, and for many global citizens today it remains the ultimate basis of their commitment to a global moral order. Whilst many thinkers would reject as the basis of their commitment to global ethic the idea of a natural law, it remains central to any conception of global citizenship that there is a global ethic of some kind. As we will see below, there are numerous ways of understanding and justifying this global ethic but the central core of a global ethic is precisely what binds together Stoic cosmopolitanism and modern cosmopolitanisms of various kinds.

The elitism of Stoicism, which not all Stoics themselves were comfortable with, does not prevent any rational person from becoming part of the wider community, since all human beings, in being rational, are capable of being wise. The exercise of reason wisely through moderation is anyway a necessary condition of full social harmony. Even if we stress that all human beings are global citizens because of a certain moral status, there is still something elitist in recognising that some human beings are global citizens *in a fuller sense* if they adopt that self-identity and become active. Although we tend to be more pessimistic about the possibility of full harmony in human relations, the goal of greater harmony is central to the efforts of global citizens. Indeed the more people become global citizens, the more likely such harmony is.

Distinctions within cosmopolitanism

Despite my stress on the continuities between Stoic cosmopolitanism and modern cosmopolitanism, we do have to accept that cosmopolitanism is a term open to a number of different interpretations. Some writers distinguish between ethical cosmopolitanism and institutional cosmopolitanism. The former is essentially the idea of a global ethic that 'every human being has a global status as the ultimate unit of moral concern' (Pogge 1992: 49), the latter the idea that 'the world's political structure should be reshaped so that states and other political units are brought under the authority of supranational agencies of some kind' (Beitz 1999: 287). This might appear to be a division between cosmopolitanism as applied to individuals and that applied to states but this would be misleading, since an ethical cosmopolitanism is a global ethic that ought to guide the behaviour of individuals *and states*. As such, someone committed to ethical cosmopolitanism may not merely be interested in what individuals ought to do in relation to one another but also engage in a critique of what states (or companies) do and act to try and change their policies. Indeed, in the sphere of international relations theory much contemporary cosmopolitanism is precisely focused on the assessment of state behaviour. Conversely, an institutional cosmopolitanism may not merely be about the restructuring of international relations or about new forms of global governance, it may be about how individual agents are to be understood in relation to such changes as politically global citizens. Much modern interest in global citizenship actually combines all four elements of cosmopolitan thinking: a strong ethical basis for both the behaviour of individuals and for the assessment of international relations combined with, as a consequence of the ethical reasoning involved, a commitment to developing new forms of global governance, including ones in which the global citizenship of individuals can be fully expressed.

GLOBAL ETHICS

I now examine the ethical basis of cosmopolitanism: what forms might this global ethic take? Although I go further into issues of ethical theory in Chapter 8, here I merely indicate several different kinds of answer: objective truth about timelessly valid norms and values; norms and values based on subjective preference; norms and values already existing as a common core; norms and values constructed by a process of consensus-building.

Objective truth

Although many modern thinkers are deeply suspicious of the idea that there are timeless objective truths about what is good and right (that any rational well-informed thinker should accept), this assumption about the nature of ethics has been, in fact, the dominant approach in Western thought and in many other traditions. Indeed, in so far as ethics is thought to be bound up with religious belief, and religious belief is thought to be about some divine *reality*, the presumption is that values themselves have the same kind of status. It is still very popular amongst both religious and non-religious thinkers. There are many varieties of such objective ethics, both in the detailed ways ethics is understood and indeed in the range of substantive normative values and norms each theorist supports. I focus here on two examples, namely Kant and Utilitarianism, though other approaches are discussed at various points. Many, though not all, advocates of human rights would adopt this approach to understanding human rights.

Immanuel Kant (1724–1804) is a good figure to focus on both because he was such a towering intellect whose thought has had such a deep influence in many areas and because he was quite self-consciously a cosmopolitan thinker. Indeed, in the context of international relations cosmopolitanism is sometimes called (misleadingly) Kantianism. As a prominent figure of the Enlightenment, Kant held that all humans possessed the power of reason and that this reason, if exercised properly, would yield essentially the same truths for all thinkers. Ethics was not excluded from this. He saw understanding and acting on our sense of duty as essentially our capacity to accept and act on 'requirements of practical reason'. This was famously called the 'categorical imperative'. The imperative came from our own reasoning powers – it was not imposed by anything outside us, like social convention, the command of a sovereign or even God. We are autonomous makers of the moral law. The categorical imperative was expressed in several ways, the two most striking being 'so act that your maxim is willed to be a universal law of nature' and 'so act that you treat humanity whether in your own person or any other person never merely as means but as an end in itself' (Kant 1949). The first formulation essentially stresses that whatever you do you must be prepared to universalise it. The second states that in any relations with people you must, since they are rational pursuers of ends, always respect them as persons. Thus, for instance, lying to, stealing from or coercing other people are wrong simply because none of these actions can be universalised and in each case you are failing to respect the rational agency of other persons.

What is important about Kant's ethical theory for our purposes is that the categorical imperative applies to our relationships to all fellow human beings as fellow rational agents. It is a global ethic. Kant explicitly recognised the cosmopolitan aspects of his ethical theory. In his seminal short work *Perpetual Peace* and elsewhere, he constructed a model of international relations that would, given the frailties of human nature, be likely to advance moral well-being. He distinguished three kinds or levels of *recht* (right): republican, international and cosmopolitan (Kant 1970b). A republican state, for Kant, is one founded on moral principles of freedom and equality, and an international order should be based on a range of 'articles of peace' that would preserve international peace and order (precisely because they are based on principles of mutual respect by republican states); cosmopolitan duty refers to the duty of hospitality towards foreigners. Whilst Kant was thinking primarily of foreigners who might visit one's own society, the principle is potentially very powerful because we have obligations towards any human being anywhere in the world and because, in addition to relations between states, there are relations between individuals across the world that are not mediated through states. In addition to this ethical cosmopolitanism, Kant had some, albeit cautious, interest in institutional cosmopolitanism as well. In another influential essay *The Idea of a Universal History with a Cosmopolitan Intent*, he envisaged the emergence of a cosmopolitan political order in the distant future – but it is distant, since, as things are, world government would be exceedingly dangerous (Kant 1970a).

Another example of a still influential traditional approach to ethics that usually sees ethics as a set of objective truths of timeless validity is Utilitarianism. Utilitarianism arose in the late eighteenth and early nineteenth centuries, particularly in the hands of Jeremy Bentham and John Stuart Mill. The central point to Utilitarianism is the promotion of what is good and reduction of what is bad or evil. In short, the ultimate principle of morality is the maximising of *utility* or the best balance of good over evil. Rightness is determined by consequences (as least those intended or reasonably foreseeable). Classically, this was expressed as the greatest happiness principle because good was equated with happiness/pleasure and bad with pain/ suffering (Mill 1962). Later writers preferred to talk about maximising the satisfaction of preferences, interests and so on. Utilitarianism does not dispense with ordinary moral rules but these rules are seen as justified precisely because they promote happiness and so on, and if following a rule on an occasion does not do this, there is reason not to follow it. The key point for us about the approach is that it is a *global* ethic (though it may not be called this normally) because our ethical thinking must take into account the interests of all those affected by our actions, and this includes those who live in other societies. Much commitment by individuals to do something for the world is motivated by Utilitarian thinking, for example Peter Singer's radical principle that challenges the affluent to alleviate world poverty (Chapter 6).

Utilitarianism is commonly presented as an example of an objectivist ethical theory that, once the prejudice of tradition and religious bias is removed, would commend itself to any reasonable agent as the right basis for ethics. Various writers have attempted to ground it in facts about human nature or rational principles of action. These claims are hotly disputed by many philosophers these days (Sen and Williams 1982; Smart and Williams 1973).

Subjectivism

Subjectivism denies that there are objective ethical truths to be 'discovered' and instead sees ethics as a function of the individual whose ethic it is – based on a person's feelings, preferences, choices or whatever. During the twentieth century, varieties of subjectivism had been very popular.

Subjectivism may be hostile to the whole idea of global ethics – particularly if it is linked to relativism, which is often advanced in criticism of universalism in ethics (see Chapter 8). But a subjectivist can present her ethical theory as a global ethic. Instead of saying, like an objectivist, 'these are the moral facts or what reason requires us to accept', she may be saying 'this is the kind of world I recommend – one in which we don't kill or deceive one another, and in which we care about one another – because I want or prefer to act and be treated by others in these ways'. An influential theory in the mid-twentieth century was R. M. Hare's theory of universal precriptivism: to make a moral judgement is to issue a universal prescription addressed to oneself and to all others in like situations (Hare 1963). This theory was subjectivist in my sense. Interestingly enough, in his later writings Hare saw his theory as supporting a form of Utilitarianism. This illustrates a more general point: a normative theory that presents certain norms like Utilitarianism may well be supported on objectivist grounds or it may be supported in others ways. Another modern philosopher, J. J. C. Smart, also provided a non-objectivist defence of Utilitarianism by seeing it as the ethical code we get if we generalise the attitude of benevolence (Smart and Williams 1973).

Pre-existing common core

We now turn to the first of two approaches to a global ethic that base the idea of a global ethic on what is accepted as norms and values in the world, rather than on what, from the thinker's point of view, ought to be accepted.

A global ethic is a set of values and norms that are, as a matter of fact, universally or generally accepted throughout the world. There is great controversy about how far there really are common values and norms throughout the world. Part of the difficulty is that if one means values and norms accepted by absolutely everyone capable of moral thought, there will be nothing in common, since individuals can hold strange views! If one means all cultures and sub-cultures, again there might be very little as a lowest common denominator. If one means values and norms that are generally (not universally) accepted, then it may be more plausible to identify a significant list. At any rate, many thinkers have tried to come up with such lists, and for many who think of themselves as global citizens some such common core is needed to make sense of the global community of which they are part, since a community seems to imply at least some common core values holding it together as a community.

The *Declaration toward a Global Ethic* of the Parliament of the World's Religions of 1993 came up with four leading ethical directives and many sub-specifications of them. The four main ones are:

> Commitment to a culture of non-violence and respect for life;
> Commitment to a culture of solidarity and a just economic order;
> Commitment to a culture of tolerance and a life of truthfulness;
> Commitment to a culture of equal rights and partnership between men and women. (Küng and Kuschel 1993)

The assumption behind this Declaration is made explicit in the writings of Hans Küng, one of the leading proponents of the Declaration, namely that there is a common core in all the world's major religions summed up in the golden rule: 'do unto others what you would have done to you' (Küng 1991; 2002). These principles are not particularly new; such a common core predates and has nothing to do with modern processes of globalisation. It may emanate from a common divine source or be no more than a reflection of the minimum requirements for social life to be possible at all, or be based on what all humans have *reason* to have or be (Alkire 2002). Such a common core needs diverse interpretation, as Alkire stresses, as well as various and new applications in the modern world.

Construction of a global ethic

Another example of an attempt to identify a common core is contained in an influential international report called *Our Global Neighbourhood*. In its second chapter, entitled significantly 'Values for the Global Neighbourhood', it noted that establishing an ethical dimension to global governance requires us to:

> Enunciate and encourage commitment to core values concerned with the quality of life and relationships, and strengthen the sense of common responsibility for the global neighbourhood;
>
> Express these values through a global civic ethic of specific rights and responsibilities that are shared by all actors, public and private, collective and individual. (CGG 1995: 48)

The values it identifies are: respect for life; liberty; justice and equity; mutual respect; caring; integrity. The elements of the global civic ethic are:

> Rights of all people to:
> A secure life;
> Equitable treatment;
> An opportunity to earn a fair living and provide for their welfare;
> The definition and preservation of their differences through peaceful means;
> Participation in governance at all levels;
> Free and fair petition for redress of gross injustices;
> Equal access to information; and
> Equal access to the global commons.
> Shared responsibility to:
> Contribute to the common good;
> Consider the impact of their actions on the security and welfare of others;
> Promote equity, including gender equality;
> Protect the interests of future generations by pursuing sustainable development and safeguarding the global commons;
> Preserve humanity's cultural and intellectual heritage;
> Be active participants in governance; and
> Work to eliminate corruption. (CGG 1995: 56–7)

Unlike the Declaration of the Parliament of the World's Religions, this statement of values, rights and responsibilities is not intended to be a statement of timeless values but rather what a very large number of actors in the world today would accept. It is an example of the way ethics emerges from changing conditions and from the necessity to co-operate to protect interests, for instance in response to common environmental threats. What is important here is not that conditions arising from living on a small planet create the necessity for norms of co-operation and mutual accommodation but that the norms emerge through processes of dialogue, consensus-building, negotiation and so on. The function of declarations, authoritative statements and charters like the Earth Charter (see Chapter 6) is precisely to consolidate and reinforce the emerging 'global ethic'. Indeed, the *Universal Declaration of Human Rights* of 1948 both asserted an emerging consensus at the time about the status of all human beings and also provided a cornerstone for further acceptance and observance of those very rights (see Chapter 4).

Such declarations and statements also illustrate another important point. However much such statements, as reflecting or strengthening an emerging consensus, represent a global ethic, they necessarily only represent part of it. In so far as a global ethic is seen as a set of values, norms, rights and responsibilities, it lacks a dimension in its background – namely theoretical justification and amplification. The founders of the *Universal Declaration of Human Rights* did not just sit down and ask: 'What rights are generally accepted in the world – let's now write them down!' They came to the process with their own views about what rights were about, which were important and how to justify them. Anyone's ethic as a set of values has a story (theory, worldview) lying behind it and it is almost certainly not the same story as those lying behind others' acceptance of the same ethic. Anyone's 'ethic' (global or otherwise) is partly constituted by the background story one accepts. For many global citizens, what makes them feel they are part of global moral community is precisely the fact that there is some common core of values and norms that they can, given their own particular background of belief and thought, for their part endorse.

In this chapter I have not compared or evaluated different approaches to global ethics or considered the reasons others have for rejection of the whole idea (see Chapter 8 and Dower 1998; 2002b; 2002c). Rather, I have illustrated how global citizenship involves a global ethics component and how that component is appropriate, either from the necessities and problems of the modern world or from ethical ideas with a long history like cosmopolitanism. Still the question may be asked: granted that we need to think in terms of a global ethic, why do we need to talk of global *citizenship*? What distinctive contribution, if any, does this idea make? Answering this is the task of the next chapter.

QUESTIONS

1. What are the main problems facing the world today? Why are they problems?
2. Does being a global citizen today have much in common with Stoic cosmopolitanism?
3. Are ethical norms timeless truths? If not, why not?
4. Looking at the list of rights and responsibilities (p. 32), which would you emphasise? Are there any you would drop or add?

---

3. CITIZENSHIP IN A GLOBALISED WORLD

SUMMARY OF KEY POINTS COVERED IN THIS CHAPTER

Citizenship
  Legal-political basis
  Political–institutional relationship
  Ethical basis
Different conceptions of citizenship
  Liberalism
  Republicanism
  Identity politics and group rights
Scholte's account of globalisation
  Deterritorialisation
  Four dimensions: production; governance; community; knowledge
Relevance of globalisation to global citizenship
  Citizenship with global concerns
  NGOs and global civil society
  Transnational solidarities: cosmopolitan and particularist
Elements of citizenship potentially replicable at global citizenship level
  Informal (for example, global civil society)
  Formal (for example, human rights regime)

CITIZENSHIP

Relevance to global citizenship

If global citizenship is to have some significance beyond that of moral agency directed to global concerns, then we need to get clearer about what the word 'citizen' entails and about how the meaning of 'global citizenship' is informed by the meaning of 'citizenship'. One possible approach is to say that its meaning is identical to that used when we talk of citizenship of the state. Citizenship in the state is or entails a formal relationship to the state. World citizenship then entails world government and the concept does not have application in the modern world.

However, the word 'citizen' may of course be used in a metaphorical sense to indicate, for instance, no more than the idea of membership of a community in which the legal and political aspects of standard citizenship are discarded. Here the word 'citizen' does some conceptual work – membership of a community – that goes beyond or at least makes explicit what 'being a moral agent with global concerns' really means. Thus, Aldo Leopold, the famous ecologist, remarks that human beings should stop seeing themselves as 'conquerors of the land-community' and see themselves instead as 'plain members and citizens of it' (Leopold 1949: 204). As later environmentalists have suggested, this is a way of thinking of global citizenship, namely *ecological* global citizenship (van Steenbergen 1994).

A third approach is that the idea of 'citizenship' has a number of strands to it and in understanding global citizenship one is picking out one or two, but not all, strands. Thus, if citizenship is partly about deliberative participation in public affairs, then that is the element relevant to global citizenship.

Again, if citizenship is itself a 'contested' concept, with different theorists advocating alternative conceptions, the advocate of global citizenship is implicitly or explicitly taking up one of the contested meanings and applying this at another level. Thus, on a certain reading of liberal citizenship the legal protection of rights is central and then extended to the global level of international human rights law.

We need then to look first at issues to do with citizenship itself. In any case, revival of interest in the idea of citizenship itself in the last fifteen to twenty years has been one of the sources of interest in global citizenship. The fact that citizenship has become an actively contested concept has opened up many issues to do with rights, identity, democracy and so on, and this has created an intellectual space in which the global dimensions of citizenship can fit it (see for example Heater 2000 and Linklater 2002). I discuss citizenship under six headings (see Summary box above).

The legal-political basis

Citizenship is a status conferred on individuals by political communities to which they belong. The paradigm of a political community in the modern world is the nation-state – sovereign bodies recognised by one another as such in the society of nation-states (though citizenship of the European Union is an example of a different kind of political community existing at the current time). At other times, the political community of which one might be 'citizen' was different. In the heyday of classical Greece, the unit was the city-state (thus the 'citi' of 'citizen' and 'polis' in 'political'). Somewhat later, during the era of the Roman Empire, people were 'citizens' of an empire.

The two main ways in which someone's citizenship at this basic level is determined are place of birth or parentage, though not all states recognise both as bases for the status of citizen. A third way of becoming a citizen is by naturalisation, that is applying to become a citizen and, subject to certain residency and/or other tests and qualifications, being accepted. Given that these three ways of having citizenship status could lead to people being citizens of more than one state, states adopt various approaches to dual or multiple citizenship. Multi-level citizenship is also possible, as with citizenship of the European Union alongside citizenship of member-states. What this already illustrates is that there is considerable legal variation in the conditions of citizenship itself. Furthermore, not all those who reside in a state are necessarily citizens of that state. It is important to note that many of the rights and duties citizens have are also conferred upon non-citizens but that, for any given political community, citizens have some rights and duties that non-citizens do not. But there is no consistency about this; non-citizens may, for instance, have rights to certain socio-economic benefits in one country that are restricted to citizens in another.

T. H. Marshall in the middle of the twentieth century identified three kinds of citizenship rights: political rights (for example, rights to political participation); civil rights (for example, rights to liberty, personal security and due legal process); and social rights (for example, rights to receive from the state various social and economic benefits). Part of his argument was that what emerged in the twentieth century was the importance of the third kind of rights, which underpinned the idea of the welfare state (Marshall 1973). Again there are variations over what rights are legally established and how, and over what citizens have that non-citizens do not have.

Citizens also have legal duties of various kinds. These include duties to obey the laws, including laws designed to protect people's rights, especially civil rights; duties to pay taxes to maintain law and order and external security, and in some countries to finance welfare provision; duties to do military service if called on to do so; and in some countries duties to vote in elections. Generally, these duties, especially the first two (obey the law and pay taxes), which constitute the standard and regular duties of citizens, are also the duties of non-citizens as well.

It is clear that whilst citizenship of a state must have some reference to some set of legal rights and duties, these are variable and provide no clear basis for distinguishing citizenship from resident non-citizenship. We need to add a less tangible but more important element.

Political–institutional relationship

Why is citizenship such an important status for someone to possess? For the individual citizen, apart from the enjoyment of certain rights, which are protected (and might not be if she was not a citizen), it is the sense of belonging to a particular political community that is the tangible social reality within which citizens conduct their lives and that shapes powerfully the nature and character of their lives. For those who are in government, a strong nation-state is supported as a distinctive political community by its citizens' loyalty, sense of belonging to and identification with it.

The form of this 'bond' may be thought of in different ways and indeed be different in different cases. Thus, a liberal may stress the state as the provider of security and rights; a republican may stress the state as expressive of one's political autonomy; a communitarian may stress the state as a political community that through its traditions and history, constitutes an important part of people's identity. To be a citizen then is to have certain psychological attitudes towards the country of one's birth, parentage or choice. In its stronger forms, it comes out in forms of patriotism and in moral priorities that accord the interests of one's own community or individuals in it a higher moral status than those of people outside it. (Citizenship is linked to patriotism rather than nationalism, which, whilst it is distinct from patriotism, sometimes supports and sometimes opposes it. Both attitudes can conflict with cosmopolitanism, as can other loyalties to social groups based on ethnicity, a sense of being a 'people' and so on: see Chapter 8.)

Ethical basis

Underlying the elements of citizenship discussed above and of relevance to global citizenship itself is an ethical basis. The state is itself usually a moral community. This is already implicit in what has been said, since the language of legal rights and duties and of law is itself normative, as indeed are the ideas of loyalty towards and identity with one's state. A legal or political system would not be legitimate if people did not accept moral reasons for obeying the law, respecting other people's rights, paying their taxes and otherwise supporting the state. Authority is the legitimate or justified exercise of power and its justification for citizens comes from their moral beliefs. Without this being true of most people, the system would either not operate or become a tyrannous exercise of mere power in which citizenship is undermined or limited.

The rights and duties I have as a citizen are rights and duties I have in relation to fellow citizens. They are not the same rights and duties as I have in relation to all fellow human beings. Even if one denied the existence of the latter rights and duties, the former would still be important. However, for a global citizen, it is important to assert the latter as well and to agree with Locke that, if an Indian and a Swiss met in the woods, they would be bound by the moral law even though they were not members of society with one another (Locke 1960: 277). How far the moral basis of my rights and duties qua citizen derives from the nature of the political order I belong to, and how far from the basis of a universal morality of humans as humans, is one of the points of division between different theories of citizenship (see also Parekh 2002).

Liberalism

Next we consider, following Hutchings, the distinction between liberal and republican conceptions (Hutchings 1999), though in fact most people's conceptions of citizenship involve elements of both (and this will be significant for the extension to global citizenship). Hutchings traces the origins of the liberal conception back to John Locke (1632–1704), whose *Second Treatise of Government* (Locke 1960) is often seen as a key text of liberalism. Locke's essential picture is that the state is a device for protecting our rights. Human beings give up their natural 'executive right of nature' – the right to punish others who transgress their rights – and hand this over to the state in return for the state's protection of them. An implication of this is that even outside the state or political community we have natural rights, that is moral rights in virtue of our nature as human beings. For Locke, these were summed up as the rights to 'life, liberty and property', though different thinkers in the liberal tradition may emphasise different things. For some modern liberals, amongst the rights to be protected are rights to welfare (socio-economic rights) (Rawls 1971), whereas others, sometimes now called libertarians, resist this and stress the rights to liberty, especially economic liberty, as paramount (Nozick 1974).

The conception of citizenship to emerge from this is somewhat passive, since being a citizen of state is being the bearer of protected rights. As Hutchings remarks, 'the powers of the state are limited and ultimately derive from the people who are governed by the requirement of natural law, but as long as the state abides by these requirements the active participation of the people in legislation and government is not necessary' (Hutchings 1999: 7).

Even if such participation is taken to be central to democracy, this does not make the liberal conception 'non-democratic'. If the point of the state is to protect the right of individuals and to do so equally (a further assumption generally made), then there must be procedures in place that both check the exercise of political power by having electorates who vote parties in and out of power and also give proper weight to the preferences of citizens (whilst providing protection for minority interests). Furthermore, if a liberal includes amongst the basic rights to be protected the right to have a say in the affairs of one's community (which in modern political communities means a right to participation in political decision-making), then some case is made for a right to have democratic procedures in place. Finally, the proper functioning of democracy as a formal device for checking power and for expressing preferences requires the active participation in public affairs of significant minorities of citizens. But the point remains that active, democratically engaged citizenship is primarily seen as an effective *means* towards the realisation of other values. This leads us to the main difference between liberal conceptions of citizenship and democracy and those of the republican.

Republicanism

As David Miller, a defender of the republican conception, notes, the republican conception goes further than the liberal conception in stressing not just rights and reciprocal duties but also the idea of citizens 'being willing to take active steps to defend the rights of other members of the political community, and more generally to promote its common interests' (Miller 1999: 62). This involves playing 'an active role in both the formal and informal areas of politics. Political participation is not undertaken simply in order to check excesses of government [. . .] but as a way of expressing your commitment to the community' (Miller 1999: 63). 'Promoting common interests', 'political participation' and 'commitment to the community' all capture the essence of the position: active involvement in the life of one's political community is the essence of citizenship. For this, certain virtues of citizenship are required, such as public spiritedness, commitment to democratic dialogue and so on. On this view, democracy is understood in a rather stronger sense as the expression of autonomy – that is, self-government – and as involving a duty (not just a right) not merely to vote from time to time but to be involved in *res publica*, that is public affairs. One of the sources of this republican conception of citizenship is Jean Jacques Rousseau (1712–78). Unlike Locke, he thought that we did not have pre-existing natural rights and that being part of a commonwealth involved a transformation of our status, since it was through the existence of the state that our rights and obligations were formed and we become both subjects and citizens, subjects qua subject to the law and citizens qua makers of the law (Rousseau 1966).

We can see here a strong element of communitarian thinking that has been attractive to a number of modern critics of liberalism, such as Sandel (1982). Our rights and duties are constituted by the community and its traditions, our identity as citizens is formed in the relationships we have with our community and, as such, we have an overall commitment to the public good of that community. However, there is no necessary connection between republicanism and communitarian thinking. First, political communitarians like Bradley (Bradley 1876) have not always been sympathetic to the republican ideals of democracy. Second, republican ideals of active democratic citizenship do not have to be premised on the view that we do not have any pre-existing moral rights or moral status prior to and independent of concrete rights and duties of actual states. Indeed, Aristotle provided a robust conception of citizenship in terms of active participation in public affairs and defined a human being as a 'political animal', meaning by this that humans most fulfilled their nature engaging in the public life of their political community. But there was no suggestion that the elements of human flourishing, including that of political participation, were socially constructed in particular communities – they were just basic facts about what made up human well-being (Aristotle 1988).

Multi-culturalism and identity politics

In recent years there has been much discussion about the inadequacies of liberal democracy and standard understandings of citizenship. The impetus for this has come from a number of sources, such as concern for racial equality, feminist concerns for sexual equality and the positions of minority groups such as ethnic or religious groups, indigenous peoples or people with non-standard sexual orientation. Many of these concerns centre round the challenge of 'multi-culturalism'. First, members of certain groups may be disadvantaged in various ways (economic status, public recognition) and feel that it is because they belong to a certain group that they are disadvantaged or discriminated against. Second, their identity as members of a certain group cannot be properly recognised unless *group* rights are recognised. People's identities as black, women, Muslim, Inuit, gay and so on are important to them – hence the idea of 'identity politics'. Democratic procedures as currently understood do not give proper weight to these considerations, since the rights of minorities (as individuals or as group) have no way of being factored into democratic decision-making. Citizenship needs to give such groups an adequate 'voice' – a term much used by feminists and multi-culturalists – so that their perspectives are adequately reflected in public policy (for example, in policies on schools). As Isin and Wood say:

> We view the relationship between citizenship and identity from a perspective that sees modern citizenship not only as a legal and political membership in a nation-state but also as an articulating principle for the recognition of group rights. We conceive of citizenship broadly – not only as a set of legal obligations and entitlements which individuals possess by virtue of their membership of a state, but also as the practices through which individuals and groups formulate and claim new rights and struggle to expand or maintain existing rights. (Isin and Wood 1999: 4)

Such perspectives cut across the traditional contrast between liberalism and republicanism. Clearly, at a theoretical level, there is a challenge to the individualism in liberalism's emphasis upon right being individuals' rights. But equally, in so far as republicanism makes much of the virtues of citizenship as commitment to public affairs and thus a specific political conception of the 'good', there is a conflict with those groups whose identities and associated ways of life are viewed as more important than the value of citizenship or of one's identity as Canadian, or whatever. I mention Canada because these issues have been much debated there, partly through the influence of the political philosopher Will Kymlicka (for example, Kymlicka 1995). If liberals interpret the right to freedom to include the rights of *groups* to live in their distinctive ways, it can to some extent accommodate these concerns. Whether the liberal conception or that of the 'participatory' republican conception can meet adequately these concerns is much discussed (see for example, Young 2000).

Applications of citizenship to global citizenship

The above accounts of citizenship provide half the background for our task of applying the idea of citizenship to global citizenship. We now need the other half of the background, namely what it is about the modern world that has made the extension of citizenship (rather than mere responsibility) to global citizenship appropriate. I give an account of the relevant changes in the world under the general heading of 'globalisation'. Apart from helping the reader to see how complex and contested a concept citizenship itself is, the survey above has prepared us for the variety of ways in which the extension to the global may be made, depending on what elements or approaches we take to be relevant.

GLOBALISATION

Following Scholte, we can identify five different ways of thinking of globalisation: internationalisation (the development of international institutions); liberalisation (the spread of the free market in the world economy); universalisation (the spread of the same images and ideas across the world); modernisation (the modern state, bureaucracy and so on); and deterritorialisation (Scholte 2000). Whilst the first four all capture aspects of the process, he argues for the latter as providing the most insight into the process, which, whilst it has been going on over the last 150 years, gained momentum in the last thirty. Deterritorialisation is the process whereby social space becomes more and more global in not being located in any particular territory. Thus, a person might belong to a global social movement of people who are spread all over the globe, who communicate across the world and whose concerns are global issues like the status of women, the plight of prisoners or the saving of a rare species. This account of globalisation makes central the role of consciousness, of how people see the world. It is not enough to think of it as a process in which things happening in one part of the world simply cause things to happen in other parts. As Spybey puts it, 'a truly globalised world [is one] in which the individual cannot avoid coming into contact with the global' (Spybey 1996: 26). Tomlinson remarks, in commenting on the Commission on Global Governance's use of the phrase 'global neighbourhood', that globalisation produces an 'enforced proximity' (Tomlinson 1999: 181).

What are the major areas in which globalisation takes place? Often when people first think of globalisation they think of economic globalisation and the role of big companies. In this sense, the protesters at Genoa in 2001 may have been anti-globalisation, though in fact they were not in other ways (see Chapter 7). Scholte identifies four major strands of globalisation: production (of which global capitalism is the chief engine); governance (in which sub-state, supra-state and non-state agencies play increasing roles, including the development of the UN system and international law); community (in which transworld solidarities are formed, as well as cosmopolitan concerns through 'global civil society'); and knowledge (where the universal rationalist paradigm – secularist, anthropocentric, scientistic, instrumentalist – contends with other paradigms but where global consciousness is an important phenomenon).

Various questions can be asked of globalisation. How far has globalisation actually taken place? It is after all the label of a *process*, not a completed state, and the process may not have got very far. Is the process on the whole a good thing or a bad thing? Is the process inevitable or can it be modified? Perhaps overall it cannot be reversed or stopped but the particular directions it takes may well be under our control. The answers to this last question are particularly important if we are to develop a robust account of global citizenship. All these questions are highly controversial and many answers are given (see Held and McGrew 2000). Here I follow Scholte in his assessment. He adopts a middle ground position between the 'globalisers' and the 'sceptics', both in respect to the issue of the extent to which globalisation has taken place and in respect to the benefits and harms caused by globalisation (see also Newlands 2002 for the effects of economic globalisation).

The impact of globalisation on state citizenship

Even before we consider the extension of citizenship to global citizenship, we can see three ways in which globalisation affects citizenship within a state.

First, minimally, citizens going about their ordinary lives without much regard for either the world or their country and only interested in realising their various rights as citizens may be affected in various ways by globalisation without even realising it. Their jobs may be affected by companies investing elsewhere. Their savings may be affected by global market trends. Regulations they have to follow may be passed in some supranational body like the European Commission in Brussels for citizens of the European Union. Structural Adjustment Programmes imposed on poor countries by the International Monetary Fund (IMF) may have effects on the life-chances of poor people if, for instance, government subsidies are removed.

Second, active citizens may become aware of the forces of globalisation and engage in political processes by lobbying, joining NGOs or political parties and so on, in order to protect their own interests or the interests of their group, or the interests of their own country, by exploiting new opportunities or trying to get round the constraints or problems being caused. The citizen takes on a global information perspective but is still motivated by the desire to protect her own, her group's or her country's interests.

Third, active citizens may acquire the same knowledge about globalisation but, because of certain moral concerns that extend beyond their own country, engage in politics in various ways, including joining political parties, lobbying MPs, working through nation-based NGOs with global concerns but who operate though applying political pressure on national governments (like the World Development Movement in the UK, see Chapter 6). Their concerns may be broad global concerns (like environmental issues) or they may be based on the interests of particular groups with which they identify (for example, women's issues) or for which they feel solidarity (for example, indigenous people).

The third case raises an interpretative issue. Is such a person better described as *a globally oriented citizen* (as Parekh calls it) or as a *global citizen*? Someone who is sceptical of the whole idea of global citizenship or who thinks that only those who actually engage in transnational organisations and institutions are really global citizens will prefer the former description, or prefer to interpret 'global citizen' as meaning no more than the former, as Parekh suggests (Parekh 2003: 44). But there are reasons for accepting the second too, since these are cases of acting from moral concerns for people elsewhere in the world moral community. Certainly, if acting through charities like Oxfam or Christian Aid (that is, not through national political channels) is seen as global citizenship in action, then exercising one's role as a national citizen in promoting global goals through political channels should be thought of in the same way. Just because it is an exercise of national citizenship does not make it not a case of global citizenship!

If, as I indicate below, individuals with global concerns do act through networks and institutions outside the state, and we are prepared to call these instances of global citizenship because of the combination of acting though institutions and having global agendas, then there is no good reason not to call globally motivated citizenship action or 'global citizen action' (Edwards and Gaventa 2001) a form of global citizenship. If significant numbers of citizens within a state do use their national political processes to advance global agendas, that already indicates an aspect of the 'global transformation' taking place, since traditionally citizenship was conceived as being primarily about participation in the public good of one's own state! One of the best hopes for cosmopolitanism is actually through re-orienting national priorities from within. This presupposes a strong and resilient state but one open to cosmopolitan influences (Falk 2002; see also Axtmann 2002).

Implications of Scholte's account of globalisation for global citizenship

Where does global citizenship fit into Scholte's account of globalisation? It is striking that the phrase 'global citizen' does not feature at all in his discussion (though its cognate 'cosmopolitanism' does feature a few times). One might think that this analysis of globalisation, like so many others that make no use of the category 'global citizenship', leaves no space, conceptually, for the idea of global citizenship. However, this would be a serious misreading. On the very last page he asserts that the move towards a more humane globalisation requires *inter alia* 'large-scale efforts to build active support for reform amongst veritable "global" citizens' (Scholte 2000: 317). Perhaps the inverted commas signals reservations but, whatever his own position, I now demonstrate how his account of globalisation provides exactly the right framework for making sense of global citizenship in the modern world.

Whilst he acknowledges that on balance the effects of globalisation on the key human values he identifies – security, justice and democracy – has been more negative than positive, because of the dominant role of neo-liberal policies, Scholte also argues for the possibility of more humane globalisation, offering a strategy of ambitious reformism with many practical suggestions, including the strengthening of the representation of non-territorial constituencies, greater consultation at the global level and strengthening of global civil society. Whilst he acknowledges five main difficulties or resistances to such change – namely the power of neo-liberal thought, persistent sovereignty, lack of institutional capacity, lack of sufficiently strong constituencies of support and the challenge of cultural diversity – the key message of his book (and this book!) is that the form globalisation takes is not inevitable and that we can make choices about its direction. This is singly the most important premise of global citizenship (or at least my conception of it) and that of most self-styled global citizens: *that individuals can make a difference, especially if they co-operate.* This is the sober optimism of global citizenship. Without it, global citizenship is either incoherent or marginalised into ineffective idealism.

In two of the four aspects of globalisation – governance and community – Scholte gives plenty of evidence of transworld social relations relevant to people being global citizens. Governance is multi-layered (being sub-state, state and supra-state), as well as involving increasing numbers of private bodies such as NGOs and economic institutions. An increasing number of NGOs play an increasing role in influencing the policy- and law-making of states and international bodies. Linked to this is the development of elements of global social democracy. If democracy is seen as 'prevailing when the members of a polity determine – collectively, equally and without arbitrarily imposed constraints – the policies that shape their destinies' (Scholte 2000: 262), then the role of the global market place, of communications and of global civil society may provide some realisation of this. This is because the world is one in which forces beyond democratic control increasingly create 'democratic deficits' even within so-called democratic states whose governments have little room for manoeuvre. People can and do influence what happens by their consumer preferences, people through the Internet can and do co-operate to promote social causes, and people through NGOs can and do advance global causes like justice, human rights and environmental protection. All this is evidence of what Falk calls 'globalisation from below' (Falk 1994; 1995). There are other aspects of global civil society that render it 'undemocratic', as Scholte notes, and the issues of how far this is the case and whether, if it is the case, it prevents us from being global citizens, will be considered in Chapter 7, along with further considerations of the contested nature of democracy itself.

In his chapter on community, Scholte is clear that amongst the non-territorial forms of community now forming, there are many transworld societies (women's movements, class solidarities, racial solidarities and so on) in which the identities such people have within these communities are quite as important as their local or state identities. Alongside these are cosmopolitan solidarities some people feel because of their concerns about global issues, such as our common environment, aid, development, human rights and sense of belonging to a universal community of mankind. In this area, several interpretative issues need to be tackled.

Particularism and cosmopolitanism

First, Scholte is at pains to distinguish global *particularist* solidarities from cosmopolitanism. Many people may get involved in some common cause like the protection of oppressed or minority groups and, of course, many do so informally through various forms of networking, or more formally through support for or active engagement within NGOs, but their concerns are not those of the cosmopolitan whose concern is with the good of the whole global community. This contrast is, however, overdrawn. For one thing, 'global civil society' is not simply a harmonious community of people all pursuing the same agendas, any more than 'civil society' is the combination of many different voluntary associations each pursuing different agendas and interests, many with a view to influencing public policies and norms. The conflicts in these agendas are, however, not *as such* conflicts between cosmopolitan concerns and particularist solidarities. In addition, the concerns to promote causes may be shaped by selfish concerns for the interests of the groups in question. Quite apart from associations like the Mafia or drug rings (which, even if we want to rule them out as part of civil society, are certainly part of globalisation and seek to influence policies to their benefit), many legally operating civil associations have private interests like stamp-collecting or specialist musical interests. But again, particularist solidarities are not generally like that.

The crucial question is: what are the main motives for these particularist social movements? Generally, those who pursue feminist agendas or those who are concerned with rectifying injustice suffered by certain classes, races, ethnic groups and other oppressed groups, do so on the basis of an implicit (if not explicit) understanding of justice for all – with some kind of cosmopolitan understanding of the basis for their particular preoccupations. Conversely, most cosmopolitan concerns focus on one or other aspect of the areas that are meant to inform a cosmopolitan order. An environmentalist is not *not* concerned with peace or human rights or poverty just because he focuses on the environment. A few cosmopolitans may want to focus on the 'big picture' and take a comprehensive view but cosmopolitanism does not require this. So if there are significant numbers of people who network, join NGOs and so on, then we have significant numbers of individuals who are, given my account of global citizenship, 'global citizens', both because of their commitment to certain global values and because they are, and see themselves as, part of real communities.

Global citizenship as an aspect of citizenship in a globalised world

What have we done in this chapter? We have not provided a proper defence of the extension of citizenship to global citizenship by addressing the various objections to such extension. We have not addressed the ethical challenge of communitarianism that the obligations that arise from membership of one's political community put limits on global obligations. Nor have we addressed critical issues surrounding the ideas of global civil society and global democracy. These issues are all addressed in Chapters 9, 8 and 7 respectively.

What we have done, by examining the various meanings of citizenship and setting out the context of globalisation, is provide an intellectual space within which it is *plausible* to draw on various elements of citizenship in order to understand global citizenship and to find empirical evidence for their replication in the transnational world. Various possibilities have emerged. Informally we can recognise:

Active participation in public affairs;

Democratic engagement in public deliberation and associated virtues of citizenship;

Membership of organisations in civil society through which the above can occur more effectively;

Membership of/belonging to a political community;

Membership of/belonging to a real moral community;

Possession of moral rights as an agreed basis for citizenship;

Adequate protection of group rights and identities.

Replication of these elements at the global level, currently existing:

The pursuit of global causes (confirmation of the purely ethical component discussed in Chapter 2);

Democratic engagement in global issues through national political parties, NGOs, networking and so on;

Membership of/belonging to a global political order, in this case through 'global civil society', for example membership of international NGOs;

Membership of/belonging to a real moral community of humankind or global neighbourhood;

Affirmation of the universal moral rights of all human beings as something widely recognised;

The development of particularist transnational solidarities for the protection of group rights and identities.

Formally, we can recognise:

Legal rights and duties through living in a political community;

Being subject to the authority of government;

A formally democratic political order (for democratic citizenship).

Replication of these at the global level has to be treated in two ways:

Currently in place: human rights regime and (embryonically) international duties of individuals;

Not currently in place but (for some) aspirational/to be worked for: formal institutions of global democracy and/or world government.

Those interested in global citizenship need not, of course, invoke all these elements in their own conceptions of global citizenship, though there is no reason not to combine many or most of them. My own particular 'inclusive' conception will be developed in the subsequent discussions. For those who prefer a formal definition of global citizenship, however, there is one element that is arguably already in place, namely international human rights. To this element of global citizenship we now turn in the next chapter.

QUESTIONS

1. Is citizenship primarily about protection of rights? If so, are group rights as important as individuals' rights?
2. Does the idea of citizenship as democratic engagement in public affairs favour the idea of global citizenship or weaken it?
3. What are the main elements of globalisation?
4. What real difference, if any, exists between a globally oriented citizen and a global citizen?
5. Looking at the list of elements of citizenship, which are most relevant to your acceptance or your rejection of global citizenship?

PART II

EXAMPLES AND AREAS OF INTEREST

4. HUMAN RIGHTS

INTRODUCTION

Human rights are relevant to global citizenship for two quite different reasons. First, much of what global citizens do is understood in terms of human rights – protecting human rights, protesting about human rights violations and so on. This is particularly so in the area of civil and political rights like protesting against detention without trial; but is also true of poverty-related work, much of which may be understood as realising the rights of the poor, rather than as simply meeting the needs of the poor or simply expressing compassion in the face of extreme suffering. Much global citizenship action is motivated by moral commitments couched in human rights terms.

Second, human rights discourse provides an important aspect of what it is to be a global citizen. Whatever else a global citizen is, a global citizen is the bearer of human rights. In saying this, we are not merely repeating the first moral claim above, we are making an existential claim about what is the case in the world. The most obvious interpretation of this is as a legal-institutional claim, that human beings have a certain status in international law, as specified in the 1948 *Universal Declaration of Human Rights*, subsequent international covenants and supporting national legal instruments. But we can also interpret this existential claim at a moral level too, to refer to commonly agreed moral norms that are widely accepted and therefore arguably part of a global moral community in which we are 'citizens'.

Human rights illustrate well the tripartite model I have introduced. Human rights provide a universal framework through which to assert the equal moral status of all human beings and a basis for those who are active in promoting or asserting the observance of human rights. Human rights constitute a legal and institutional framework in which global citizenship is now embodied in the world. Concern for human rights is usually driven by an aspirational desire to strengthen the international human rights regime, not least in respect to making more robust the mechanisms specifying the obligations of international bodies, national governments and also individuals.

I said above 'human rights provide a universal framework through which to assert the equal moral status of all human beings'. This may have struck the reader as unnecessarily complicated. Why not just say 'human rights assert the equal moral status of all human beings'? My reason for not saying this is that we need to cover two groups of moral thinkers: first, those who see their global ethic as a *theory* of moral human rights (for example, in the natural rights tradition explained below), and second, those who have a different ethical theory but who nevertheless support an international human rights regime because it gives effective expression to the universal values they do believe in. Thus, some Christians might prefer a theory/theology based on the brotherhood of humankind and the golden rule ('do unto others as you would be done unto yourself') and see human rights regimes as vitally important *in practice*. Likewise, a Utilitarian who believes in maximising human well-being might well reject human rights as a basic moral claim (indeed Bentham ridiculed it as 'nonsense on stilts') but nevertheless see the establishment of such legal and conventional practices as the best way to maximise human well-being. I outline a human rights global ethic in the next section not because I think that all global citizens subscribe to it but because many do and because it provides another example of a global ethic to set beside Kantianism and Utilitarianism as discussed in Chapter 2.

I also said above that the active element of engaged global citizens involves 'promoting and asserting the observance of human rights'. The latter verb 'asserting' is, in fact, very important. To have a right is not merely a matter of having a passive status in which you sit back and leave it to others to respect, protect or advance it. To have a right is to have something to be claimed, asserted and if necessary fought for. We need to be careful not to slip into a model in which active global citizenship is all about defending other people's rights, well-being and so on somewhere else in the world, and passive global citizenship is about having human rights and a moral status that others elsewhere do something about. Since most active global citizens who take on global responsibility tend to be from rich white Northern elites, the idea of the active global citizen asserting her rights (like the women in India hugging trees in the Chipko movement to protect their environment) helps correct this impression. Many of the global citizens in the poor South who protest against their life-conditions are just as active as those supporting them in the North. The status of bearing human rights (legal and moral) provides a form of empowerment. Indeed, there is a current Oxfam project that conceptualises global citizenship as an entitlement in the sense that learning to become an active assertive global citizen aware of one's status in international law is something that benefits someone. They therefore talk of entitlement to global citizenship education (Oxfam 2001). Although the opportunities for active self-conscious global citizenship are obviously greater in the North than in the South, the propriety of such an active status is equally so in any part of the world. Unless we can present the case for active global citizenship in this way, we are open to accusations of cultural imperialism and paternalism.

HUMAN RIGHTS AS MORAL THEORY

The basic idea

A human right is a right (a) attributed to a human being as a human being and (b) asserted to exist on the basis of a moral theory or moral reasoning. As Feinberg put it: 'I shall define "human rights" to be generically moral rights of a fundamentally important kind held equally by all human beings unconditionally and unalterably' (Feinberg 1973: 3). A human right is an important *kind* (genus, hence 'generically') of moral right, since not all moral rights are ones that all human beings have. They relate to important aspects of human well-being and apply to all human beings irrespective of local conditions. A human right is contrasted to a legal or conventional right, which exists in virtue of the laws and conventions of a given society: people have such rights as members of a legal community or whatever, not as human beings. A human right cannot be taken away by the decisions or actions of other people.

A human right exists in virtue of a universal moral theory that postulates the whole world as one moral sphere or community. A theory of human rights is therefore opposed to any form of cultural relativism that denies universally applicable values (see Chapter 8 for discussion of this). Human rights in this sense do not depend on positive law, even international law. Even an international declaration like the UN *Universal Declaration of Human Rights* neither establishes the existence of human rights nor limits what are, ethically, human rights. Thus, a right to conscientious refusal – that is, a right to refuse to do military service and train to kill – may be thought of by a theorist as a human right before it is encoded in international law. In fact, in 1993 the UN Human Right Committee in a Comment on Article 18 of the UN 1966 Covenant on Civil and Political Rights recognised it as *implied* by freedom of conscience (United Nations 1994: GEN/1/Rev. 1 at 35), though this is disputed and largely ignored by many regimes.

Its justification

How is such a position justified? Vincent contrasts four kinds of justification for rights claims: custom, positive law, contract and moral reason. Many legal and conventional rights are justified in one of the other three ways but human rights need to be justified by rational reflection. 'It is at the level at which what is appealed to is not any kind of positive law, but what ought by some rational calculation to prevail' (Vincent 1986: 11). There are various ways a moral theory of human rights can be developed. Here I merely indicate briefly several approaches.

The traditional basis of thinking of human rights, or 'the rights of man' as they were called earlier, was to think of them as natural rights – that is, rights that we have in virtue of our nature as human beings. This reflects the earlier natural law tradition of the Stoics and much Catholic moral theology according to which there is a law of our nature, the first principle of practical reasoning being to seek good and shun evil. Every human being is required to seek the elements of his well-being (life itself, reproduction, social relations and rational activity) and that of others. In so far as each person should seek this in another, the latter person has, it came to be understood, a right to that good. By the time Locke was writing in the seventeenth century, these rights were seen to be rights to life, liberty and property, which were seen as God-given rights along with duties in others to respect them. Locke conceived of these rights as rights we simply knew through the light of reason.

Whilst early talk of natural rights was clearly anchored in theological premises, later thinking about moral rights was not. Whether they are thought of as natural rights or merely universal moral rights, various attempts are made to ground these rights in certain facts about human nature, the demands of practical rationality or the conditions of human action. Mackie saw rights as the only way to shore up the idea of the equal moral status of human beings (not to be sacrificed for the greater good of others) and Gewirth developed a complex theory grounding the rights to freedom and material well-being in the conditions of human agency, arguing that we cannot make sense of distinctive human agency unless we suppose that each person has a right to choose how to act (freedom) and a right to conditions of effective action (sufficient material resources) (Mackie 1984; Gewirth 1978).

The basic rights and their correlative duties

Henry Shue has developed an influential theory of universally applicable basic rights (which are really human rights, though he does not call them such). He does not so much argue directly for them as postulate them as the precondition of the enjoyment of any other goods or rights. His theory is interesting because of the way he sets out the three basic rights and their correlative duties. He identifies the three basic types of rights as the right to subsistence, the right to security and the right to liberty (Shue 1996a). Subsistence is the basic wherewithal to continue to exist, such as adequate food, shelter, clothing, and conditions of health. Security is security of the person in being free from attack on one's person (threat to life, injury, rape and arbitrary arrest) and one's property. Liberty is the ability to give expression to one's choice free from the coercion of others (though, since it is basic, it does not as such entail political freedom and so on).

To assert that people have rights is generally to assert that others have duties or obligations in relation to those rights. Who has these duties? At one level, the answer to this question regarding human rights is easy: everyone! Such rights are often regarded as *in rem*, meaning that all other agents have duties to respect the rights in question. But in practice this leaves things unclear, particularly when it comes to the legal implementation of human rights, which requires determination of who the responsible duty-holders are. Shue's insight is to specify three types of duties corresponding to all three of these basic rights. All basic human rights have three correlative duties: duties to *avoid* depriving, duties to *protect* from standard threats of deprivation and duties to *aid* the deprived. This sounds rather forbiddingly formal but the idea is straightforward enough. If I have, for instance, a right to security, all others have a duty not to undermine my security be attacking me, robbing me and so on. But in an organised society, measures can and ought to be taken to protect people from arbitrary attack (by wrongdoers) by having effective law and order in place. Such measures cannot be foolproof, so we also have a duty to come to the aid of those who are deprived by the wrongdoing of others. The same thing can be said of the rights to subsistence and liberty.

This is to be contrasted with (and is an improvement on) the more traditional way of thinking of human rights, which assumed a big distinction between negative and positive rights. Negative rights or 'rights of action' were essentially rights to liberty (and security), in that the duty correlating with them was the duty on the part of others to refrain from violating them, and positive rights or 'rights of recipience' were socio-economic rights, e.g. to receive benefits of various kinds and this requires, as a duty, the active intervention of the state or other agents to realise these rights. If we adopt Shue's analysis, this contrast is false. Economic rights involve duties not to deprive, just as liberty rights involve duties to come to aid of those deprived of their liberties.

Implications for international relations

Two premises are essential to establishing that human rights assertions have significant implications for international relations. (a) Basic rights are 'everyone's minimum reasonable demands upon the rest of humanity' (Shue 1996a: 19). This is put in human rights terms by Luban as follows: 'Human rights are the demand of all of humanity on all of humanity' (Luban 1985: 209). If human rights are universally applicable, they entail in principle universal obligations, that is cosmopolitan responsibility. (b) If all human beings have obligations to one another, then governments ought, in their foreign as well as domestic policies, to further the realisation of human rights. If universal human rights are accepted, how far can their impact be denied or resisted by international actors? Hedley Bull, writing in the 1970s, claimed 'the framework of international order is inhospitable [. . .] to the demands of human justice' (Bull 1977: 83). (By 'human justice' he meant appeal to human rights.) But by the end of the twentieth century the climate had changed; appeal to human rights was increasingly providing a basis for humanitarian intervention and such arguments were no longer standardly trumped by appeal to the right of sovereignty (see Chapter 8). At least three factors were responsible for this: the easing of international relations since the end of the Cold War in 1989, the strengthening of human rights law and an increasing interest in cosmopolitan thinking in general and human rights thinking in particular.

There are two respects in which appeal to human rights has these implications for international relations. First, it implies the acceptance of direct obligations to further the realisation of human rights in other countries through, for instance, aid/better trade, and to play one's part in protecting a global common good such as the environment (see Chapter 6). Here the obligation arises partly because other countries actually want one to do this. Second, it implies increasing acceptance of obligations to take action to prevent/stop/discourage other countries from violating human rights within their own borders. Whilst many global citizens may have reservations about the use of military intervention to deal with human rights violations (for example, in Kosovo in 1999), the mere fact that such action for humanitarian reasons is now regarded as a serious option indicates the powerful effect that human rights thinking – not just at the legal level – has had on the way we conceive of what happens to fellow human beings elsewhere in the world. (See for example, Vincent 1986 chs 7 and 8; Luban 1985.)

HUMAN RIGHTS LAW

Universal Declaration of Human Rights

Although there had been much thinking about the possible development of international law to do with human rights for many years before, the great landmark in the establishment of human rights law at the international level was the *Universal Declaration of Human Rights*, adopted and proclaimed by the General Assembly of the United Nations on 10 December 1948. The idealism it expressed in the face of the recent atrocities of the Second World War was reflected in the Preamble:

> Whereas recognition of the inherent dignity and of the equal and inalienable rights of all members of the human family is the foundation of freedom, justice and peace in the world, Whereas disregard and contempt for human rights have resulted in barbarous acts which have outraged the conscience of mankind . . .

It contains thirty articles, most of which specify different rights. Although there are some references to obligations and to what people shall not be deprived of, not much is made of the correlative obligations and who or what institutions are to implement them, and later thinkers have wanted to supplement it with a corresponding *Declaration of Human Responsibilities*. (Such a document was promoted by the InterAction Council in 1997.) Nevertheless, there is a firm assumption about correlative duties. Although sometimes the Declaration has been accused of Western bias, it is a Declaration signed not only by the original countries in 1948 but by all countries that have joined the UN since. A product of compromise, as all international documents are, it has provided a good basis for the later developments of human rights international law. The text is given in Appendix 1 and the reader is recommended to read it through next, if it is unfamiliar.

The Declaration was a remarkable achievement. It was the first time the world had a single international legal instrument specifying the rights of all human beings. Whether or not one accepted human rights as a moral theory, it represented a gigantic step forward for anyone who did believe that there were universal human values and that they needed protecting. However, in itself it was remarkably weak. It was only a declaration and, as such, only had declaratory force, not binding force. In other words, its force was effectively a moral force encouraging states and others to observe its norms. There were no legal penalties for states that failed to observe them. Nevertheless, the Declaration and the growing momentum of support for its perspective have resulted in many subsequent developments that have created a much more robust legal framework.

Subsequent developments

We can identify a number of significant developments. (a) First and foremost, work started fairly soon after 1948 on converting the Declaration into human rights law that would be binding on member-states who ratified it. Eventually, two Covenants were agreed in the General Assembly of the UN in 1966, the *Covenant on Civil and Political Rights* and the *Covenant on Social, Economic and Cultural Rights*, both of which became binding law some years later once enough states had ratified them (United Nations 1966). (b) Parallel to the development of international law was the development of regional human rights law, such as the *European Convention on Human Rights* (Council of Europe 1950) and the incorporation of human rights into the domestic legislation of many countries (often referred to as bills of rights, which are essentially human rights if premised on the idea of universal rights). (c) Parallel to these development have been the development of human rights laws dealing with specific types of rights, like *The UN Convention on the Rights of the Child* (United Nations 1989) and the *Declaration on the Right to Development* (United Nations 1986), which attempted to formalise the obligations of rich countries to meet the development rights of poor countries but has not, to date, led to anything with binding covenant status. (d) The idea that individuals are also *subjects* of international law not merely *objects* within countries that are subjects – the view generally held in 1948 – has gained favour over the last fifty years. This is evidenced by the greater willingness to intervene in other countries' affairs for the sake of human rights and by the possibility of individuals taking cases to international courts (rarely exercised). Related to this is the development of the idea that individuals can be guilty of 'crimes against humanity' or war crimes, that is crimes in international law (not just national law) with the possibility of trial before an international tribunal. The development of an International Criminal Court is the latest expression of this idea (see last section of this chapter).

Civil and political rights v. social and economic rights?

The fact that there were two Covenants on human rights reflects a deep division that is often felt to exist, as I noted in the previous section, between the two types of rights. Although officially all parties accepted both of them, the *Covenant on Civil and Political Rights* very much represented the liberal perspective of Western countries and the other Covenant reflected the socialist perspective of the Soviet Union, which made less of civil and political freedoms as understood by the West and claimed that its system was much better at realising social and economic rights. (In fact, most Western countries had certainly had some interest in the latter, since most at that time had welfare state arrangements.) Even as late as 1975, Jimmy Carter, the then US president, could proclaim the USA as *the* champion of human rights – meaning the liberal vision of civil and political rights. Even today, people's concerns about human rights issues tend to be about civil rights and political rights, for example the defence of civil liberty, detention without trial, treatment of refugees, suppression of or denial of democratic expression. In many ways, this is unfortunate. As one writer once remarked, 'human rights begin with breakfast' (Madely 1982: 2–4). Nowadays, though, the separation is not generally accepted, at least in theory. Since the Vienna Declaration of 1993, it is usually assumed that all human rights are 'indivisible'. This does not mean that they do not sometimes clash but that they are interdependent and need to be considered holistically.

Mutual Implications?

What are the mutual implications of human rights discourse and global citizenship discourse? Does someone who believes in human rights have to believe that we are global citizens? Does someone who believes that we are global citizens have to believe in human rights? Clearly not. Many who use the one discourse do not use and do not see the need to use the other. I do not mean merely that it has not occurred to them that they could and should use it but that, given what they mean by each phrase, there may or may not be any entailment. For instance, someone who thought that legal rights were central to citizenship might hold that global citizenship certainly required international human rights law but did not require us to accept human rights moral theory. Someone who believed in human rights as a theory might well see the importance of human rights law to realise those rights but not see the latter as either sufficient for or relevant to the idea of global citizenship, which, for him, is about participation in political institutions. There are, in fact, many permutations possible here and the interested reader may like to ponder further possibilities.

Given the conception of global citizenship I am developing, it is clear that human rights theory provides one (but only one) kind of ethical background, so global citizenship does not entail a belief in human rights theory. Human rights law, however, is an essential ingredient of global citizenship. Some writers like Neff have doubted whether such law is sufficient to make the claim that we are global citizens (Neff 1999; see Chapter 9) but here I merely invoke an important element of ordinary citizenship discussed earlier, namely that *citizenship* is about bearing legally established rights and correlative duties. If we stress rights as rights possessed by all human beings, and citizenship is about the holder of rights, then global citizenship is about having these rights in a global society (whether or not people recognise or claim them and whether or not these rights are respected in their own states). This is an adaptation of T. H. Marshall's view of citizenship, as we saw earlier (Marshall 1973), as being about various categories of rights (political rights, civil rights and, he argued, characteristic of modern democracies, social rights to receive various kinds of benefits). Membership of this global legal community is not merely about rights but also about duties to respect those rights – duties that have long been recognised in principle but only recently given more active expression in war crimes tribunals and moves to set up an international criminal court.

The connection with active global citizenship is less close. Many active global citizens invoke human rights theory in promoting what they do, or use, appeal to and seek to develop international human rights law. But there again many do not, preferring other forms of moral justification and other channels of active engagement. In practice, the international human rights framework is important. First, agents assert their rights and do so in the knowledge of, and empowered by their knowledge of, the fact that these rights are human rights established in international law with correlative duties to respect and protect rights. Second, active responsibility to promote the conditions in which human rights flourish (and to oppose what thwarts these) is exercised through the appropriate institutions of global civil society. It is almost inconceivable that global civil society could fail to operate partly through the human rights framework. But these are empirical connections. Only if the right to political participation were formally established through some form of cosmopolitan democracy would active global citizenship and human rights law come closer together.

EXAMPLES

In the remainder of this chapter we will look at two examples of human rights activism and the development of the thinking behind the International Criminal Court. The examples are chosen because they represent organisations that mainly focus on a cluster of rights that can be seen as civil rights, particularly those rights that are actively violated by the deliberate actions of others, such as torture, detention without trial, judicial murder and forms of deliberate oppression. This is not to implicitly downgrade or marginalise other kinds of rights such as political rights or socio-economic rights: we discuss political rights in Chapter 7. Here I merely note that the absence or severe limitation of political rights in a non-democratic or supposedly democratic country is generally accompanied by violence, intimidation and other violations of *civil* rights. Socio-economic rights will be discussed, with examples, in Chapter 6. The promotion and protection of them is characteristically different, in that although sometimes economic rights can be actively violated by deliberate oppression, usually the massive failure of millions of people to realise these socio-economic rights is a function of natural circumstances, broad economic forces and so on.

The kinds of rights that self-consciously styled 'human rights' organisations tend to deal with are so fundamental to human decency that they cut across the traditional divide between those who advocate civil and political rights and those who advocated socio-economic rights. As Luard noted, the right to security is neither a liberty right nor a subsistence right and has been generally recognised in almost all societies, past and present (Luard 1981: 20).

Amnesty International

Amnesty International was launched in 1961 by the British lawyer Peter Benenson. Now it has more than a million members, subscribers and regular donors in more than 140 countries and territories. There are more than 7,500 local, youth and student, and professional Amnesty International groups registered at the International Secretariat (which itself has 320 staff and over 100 volunteers from more than 50 countries) (Amnesty International 2002).

Although Amnesty International supports and has in recent years become increasingly concerned about the whole range of human rights specified in the *Universal Declaration of Human Rights*, it has itself a precise mandate detailed in an international statute. The main focus of its campaigning is to:

> Free all prisoners of conscience. These are people detained anywhere for their beliefs or because of their ethnic origin, sex, colour, language, national or social origin, economic status, birth or other status – who have not used or advocated violence;
> Ensure fair and prompt trials for political prisoners;
> Abolish the death penalty, torture and other cruel, inhuman or degrading treatment of prisoners;
> End extra-judicial executions and 'disappearances'. (Amnesty International 2002)

The activity for which Amnesty International is most known is its letter-writing campaigns, where countless individuals are asked to write to government representatives in countries other than their own to try and get the release, for instance, of a particular 'prisoner of conscience'. But its activities are wide-ranging, in that it also organises demonstrations, human rights education and concerts, and does all these things not just for the sake of individual prisoners but in pursuit of particular causes, such as the abolition of torture or to highlight the issue of child-soldiers. It was also one of the founding members of the Coalition for an International Criminal Court.

Human Rights Watch

Human Rights Watch started in 1978 as Helsinki Watch, in order to 'monitor the compliance of Soviet bloc countries with the human rights provisions of the Helsinki Accords' (Human Rights Watch 2002). But it quickly broadened its base to include human rights abuses anywhere in the world, including the USA. It is the largest human rights organisation based in the United States and has more than 150 professionals working around the world outside its home base. These include academics, lawyers, journalists and experts from many countries with diverse backgrounds. The organisation often joins forces with human rights groups from other countries to further common goals such as the ICC. What it says about itself on the website is significant:

> WHY – Human Rights Watch believes that international standards of human rights apply to all people equally, and that sharp vigilance and timely protest can prevent the tragedies of the twentieth century from recurring. At Human Rights Watch, we remain convinced that progress can be made when people of good will organise themselves to make it happen. [. . .]

> HOW – The hallmark and pride of Human Rights Watch is the even-handedness and accuracy of our reporting. To maintain our independence, we do not accept financial support from any government or government-funded agency. We depend entirely on contributions from private foundations and from individuals like you. Please join thousands of other concerned *global citizens* [my italics] in supporting the work of Human Rights Watch. Together, we can make a difference. (Human Rights Watch 2002)

Some observations

Although the concerns of Human Rights Watch are broadly similar to those of Amnesty International, there are some significant differences (apart from sheer size). Whereas Amnesty International is a fully international NGO, Human Rights Watch is a national NGO that operates in many countries. Its method of operation is significantly different in that it is less of a broad-based people movement and one based more on experts who collect evidence with which to 'embarrass' governments. These factors do not make it any less appropriate a vehicle through which global citizenship can be expressed. Indeed, it invites 'concerned global citizens' to support it.

An organisation does not have to be 'international' to be part of global civil society. It is what it is about, how it relates to people and other organisations that makes it so. Part of the change that the deterritorialisation of social space is bringing about is the increasing irrelevance of formal boundaries implied by the terms 'national' and 'international'. Nor does it matter whether it is primarily experts who do the work or larger constituencies of concerned people, like Amnesty International's letter-writers. Experts are no less global citizens for being experts or being in positions others do not and cannot occupy.

Amnesty International's work with individual prisoners stands in sharp contrast to activism directed to some grand global cause such as global social justice or reduction of global warming. Indeed, Bull saw them as quite distinct – human justice and world justice (Bull 1977). This is not, however, a reason for not seeing such work as that of global citizens. An aim may be as particular as you like but if the reason appeals to some universal value, like the humane treatment of prisoners, global values are being advanced precisely through the focused activity. Likewise, if someone 'adopts a child' in another country to show global solidarity through this particular case (rather than merely through private affection), she is an active global citizen.

An important aspect of many such organisations is the influence they exert not just in getting countries to observe human rights law but in developing international law and the mechanisms for effective compliance. That is, there is progressive or aspirational element to their work.

Whilst critics may be sceptical about how effective such organisations are (wondering whether certain campaigns are counter-productive), that issue is not really our concern here. Whether or not such NGOs are always effective, they are clearly part of global civil society and they are clearly organisations through which global concerns are expressed. We may disapprove of what active global citizens do for a variety of reasons – being a global citizen is not necessarily being a good global citizen.

International Criminal Court

The international community adopted the *Rome Statute of the International Criminal Court* on 17 July 1998. The Rome Statute provided for the creation of a permanent international criminal court that would be able to prosecute people accused of genocide, crimes against humanity and war crimes. Its establishment could only proceed when 60 states had ratified the treaty. Whilst the latter happened in 2002, there was nothing inevitable about this, since governments always drag their feet when it comes to ratifying international covenants. The 1,000-strong Coalition for an International Criminal Court had been active in lobbying governments to ratify it.

As the Amnesty International website indicates, the Court will be of particular importance because:

> It will serve as a permanent deterrent to people considering these crimes. In most cases in the last fifty years international mechanisms to prosecute people accused of these crimes have only been set up after the crimes have occurred;
> It will have a much wider jurisdiction than the International Criminal Tribunals for the former Yugoslavia and Rwanda, the tribunals have been limited to crimes committed in a particular territory while crimes committed in other territories have not been addressed. (Amnesty International 2002)

According to Amnesty International, 'the treaty has been hailed by governments, legal experts and civil society as the most significant development in international law since the adoption of the United Nations Charter'. Why is this so? Ever since the Nuremberg trials after the Second World War, in which senior Nazis were tried for war crimes and crimes against humanity, the idea that individuals might be prosecuted not just for breaking national laws but for breaching international norms, whether formalised or not, has gained acceptance and is evidenced in war crimes tribunals in relation to Rwanda, Bosnia and recently Kosovo, with the trial of Slobodan Milosovic. The arrest in 1998 of General Pinochet for crimes committed in Chile when he was president and the subsequent legal process also illustrate the same point and the recognition that holding high office is no bar to the possibility of prosecution. But in each of these cases the arrangements have been ad hoc and, as such, lack the authority of universal procedures. The International Criminal Court changes all this, since it is a permanent dimension to international law.

The Court's importance for global citizenship may not be initially obvious but in fact it reinforces an aspect of citizenship at the global level. If one way of thinking of citizenship is in terms of a citizen having certain legally established rights and duties, then what the establishment of the Court does is provide a formalisation of the duties individuals have in relation to one another in the world qua members of a global legal community (see Crocker 1998). Even a crime within a country can now be conceptualised in a different way. Although, of course, the legal framework surrounding human rights already provided various kinds of protection and duties, this development has reinforced the possibility that individuals can be prosecuted, at least for the most serious kinds of human rights violations. It only represents a small part of a proper obligation framework, and there is a long way to go, but it does at least symbolise an important dimension of citizenship in the world. No doubt a defendant before the Court would not like to think of himself as a global citizen but that it what he is. The label will mean more to those whose rights are violated, and international lawyers like Richard Goldstone may well see themselves as active global citizens in making the Court work for human rights.

QUESTIONS

1. Is the best way to think of a global ethic in terms of human rights?
2. Are we global citizens in virtue of there being internationally established human rights?
3. Which rights in the *Universal Declaration of Human Rights* do you find most important?
4. In what ways do the cases of Amnesty International and Human Rights Watch illumine the idea of global citizenship for you?

---

5. PEACE AND SECURITY

SUMMARY OF KEY POINTS COVERED IN THIS CHAPTER

Framework
  Negative conception of peace: absence of war
  Positive conception of peace: harmony
  Security: range of values involved
  Importance of peace as precondition of other goods
Relevance to global citizenship
  Peace as a global value
  Precondition of human rights
  Assertion of right to peace
  Forms of activism
Peace activism
  Peace movements in the nuclear era
  World Court Project: role of 'declarations of public conscience'
  World Court opinion: generally opposed to nuclear weapons
  Trident Ploughshares: civil disobedience
  Invoking of World Court opinion
Attitudes toward foreign policy
  Various approaches possible
  Rejection of realism
  Rejection of internationalism
Promoting peace
  Cosmopolitan education: Nussbaum's four reasons
  Knowledge and values
Respecting diversity in a multi-cultural world
  Küng: no world peace without peace among the religions
  Common core and various source stories
  Limits to diversity

THE SETTING

The connection between global citizenship and peace

If, in the twentieth century before the 1970s, someone asked what being a global citizen was all about, the chances were (if the idea was congenial at all) that the answer would have had something to do with working for peace: getting involved in 'banning the bomb' or campaigning for general disarmament or for world government as the key to world peace. Since then, issues like world poverty, the environment and human rights have come to be of active concern to global citizens; and since the end of the Cold War in 1989, the threat of nuclear annihilation has receded in popular consciousness (though it has certainly not gone away).

Concerns about peace issues remain active amongst many globally-oriented thinkers and actors. In respect to the continuing threat of nuclear war, we will consider two examples – the World Court Project and Trident Ploughshares. But just as significant are other areas of active concern to do with peace and security – such as concerns focused on the proliferation of arms (opposed by, for instance, the Campaign Against the Arms Trade), anti-personnel weapons (landmines) and the use of child soldiers, and general concerns about creating the conditions of peace – in creating mutual understanding and respect between different cultures and religions, and strengthening international law and cosmopolitan education.

The negative and positive conceptions of peace

What is peace? First, there is what is called the 'negative' conception – negative not because it is unimportant or unsatisfactory but because it is seen as the negation/absence of its opposite, namely war or (more generally) active violence. In this sense, peace is a minimal relation between different human beings or groups of human beings. Such a relation may last for a short period of time and is usually of more value the longer it lasts (for some thinkers the ideal state being one of 'perpetual peace'). It exists when there is no war or active violence between the parties involved. Peace in the 'positive' conception is regarded as a state of harmony or wholeness, 'shalom' or a set of peaceful relationships between people and groups characterised by love, mutual respect, sense of justice or lack of fracture (Macquarrie 1973; Curle 1981). Whilst the achievement of peace in the negative sense has practical priority, peace in the stronger, ideal sense is usually a difficult, if not impossible, state to attain, at least on a large scale. Nevertheless, the personal expression of and advocacy of this positive ideal by those who promote peace (including those with a commitment to pacifism) may be seen as an important means of achieving widespread peace of the more limited, 'negative' kind.

Peace as a 'process' is an important means to peace as a goal (Bailey 1996); this illustrates Gandhi's idea that 'the means are the ends in the making' (see Gruzalski 2001).

Security

Security, though often coupled with peace, is somewhat different (see for example, Dower 1995). It indicates not so much a relationship between people as a condition of a person in which someone has and will continue to have the goods that are valuable to her and believes that she has and will continue to have them. She is secure both in the sense that these goods are not actually threatened now or in the relevant period of the future, nor perceived to be by her, so that she has confidence that the things she values are free from threat. In this sense, peace in one's own society and international peace (including freedom from terrorist attack) may be amongst the things that one wishes to be secure in. But so may one be about many other things – environmental security, economic security and health security, amongst others. The enjoyment of security in this broad sense is one of the central values we are concerned with (Scholte 2000: ch. 9). There may be disagreements over which aspects of security should take precedence where they cannot all be achieved. There are certainly profound disagreements about how to achieve one of the main security goals we have, namely national and international peace, and on this, as we note in several contexts, many global citizens may simply have to agree to differ.

Why peace in the negative sense is important

Thomas Hobbes, the 'father of modern political philosophy', argued in *Leviathan* in 1651 that human beings have good reason to seek peace because in a state of nature (outside organised society), which was a state of war, the life of man would be 'solitary, nasty, brutish and short' (Hobbes 1991: ch. 13). Indeed, for Hobbes it was a fundamental rational 'law of our nature' to seek peace. That is why submitting to a sovereign in a political community is the rational thing to do (or accept, since most of us find ourselves in one anyway!). Hobbes' solution to the problem of insecurity was to propose a coercive state that forced individuals to comply with the rules necessary for peaceful relations.

We need not accept his view that peace is achieved by coercion or his pessimistic analysis of relations between states (which, for him, could not be anything but warlike, given their independence and freedom from coercion by a higher 'common power') in order to gain from his insights. His reasons for regarding peace as vital are telling. If we have reason to continue to *live*, we both need to be free from personal attack and need to have continued access to what we need to continue to live – at the basic level, food, shelter and so on. We need therefore security in our possessions, which can only occur if we have entitlement to them under stable 'property' law. Without a stable, ordered society, there will be no or very little commerce or division of labour and thus very little possibility of long-term projects or co-operation – thus, the conditions of life will be wretched, lacking too all the advantages of the arts and culture.

Hobbes was imagining an extreme condition of a 'war of all against all' but still the line of argument establishes that peace is the precondition of almost all other goods and values. To put it in the form of a continuum argument: the more relations between people are based on peace and social order, the more such goods are generally achieved. Although some individuals may actually gain from war (and may even regard violence as a positive value), most people do not, as we can see from the suffering that most ordinary people experience when caught up in civil wars. Civil wars are perhaps the most obvious example of how normal human goods are destroyed, threatened and undermined; but more generally, war between states, criminal violence and terrorist violence does so as well. Conditions of peace are therefore vital to the enjoyment of most other human goods but, because they are generally in the background, they are not seen as vital until they are threatened or destroyed.

The relevance of peace to the idea of global citizenship

Given the multi-layered approach to global citizenship in this book, we can see the relevance of peace to global citizenship in a variety of ways.

First, what is characteristic of the perspective of global citizenship is that peace matters anywhere in the world because of its value to people anywhere in the world. We can distinguish this from two attitudes. (a) Someone might well be concerned about war and conflicts in other parts of the world and take or recommend action to ease such tensions but be motivated by concerns about how, if such conflicts continued or escalated, his own interests or those of his country might be negatively affected; he might get sucked into war, his economic activities might be impeded and so on. (b) Someone might recognise that peace is a universal value in the sense that for each person or group peace matters but only be concerned with peace for himself or his own country, leaving others to look after their own problems. The kind of global ethic a global citizen has goes beyond mere universalism. Whether or not he is an activist, for him it matters that people in distant places die in wars and so on. This is part of the deterritorialisation of social consciousness that makes this kind of mental 'solidarity' increasingly accepted.

Second, in so far as these goods are seen as goods we have a right to, and a right that is embodied in international legal human rights, then peace is vitally important as a means to the real enjoyment of global citizenship rights. The right to peace might also be regarded as a human right itself, though this is not so often asserted.

Third, active engagement as global citizens may take the form of claiming their rights to peace, or at least trying to achieve conditions of peace as essential to the enjoyment of other human rights they claim. Thus, people caught up in an armed conflict may try and mediate to reduce the conflict that is undermining their own lives. Likewise, many activists in the peace movement see what they are doing as not merely a duty to help create world peace but as asserting their own right not to live under the threat of nuclear annihilation.

Fourth, what is most common is active engagement by global citizens in promoting peace either locally, globally or elsewhere in the world where there is conflict. 'Being actively concerned with peace' takes many social forms and involves many diverse views about what is right or appropriate. The image of 'peace activists' chained to the gates of a nuclear base may be one image of a global citizen committed to peace; but so may be the images of a committed lawyer championing changes in international law or a person quietly thinking, meditating on or praying for peace (as the 'million minutes for peace' movement of the Brahma Kumaris urged people to do in 1986).

Varieties of active promotion of peace

Global citizenship may be expressed through a wide variety of activities:

1. Activities as citizens of one's own country devoted to peace in one's own country, such as supporting respect for multi-cultural diversity, mutual understanding, the use of dialogue, negotiation and consensus-building.

2. The private activities of individuals (who do what they do because they consider themselves as members of a world community or as promoting global causes). For instance:

   developing and maintaining personal links (like penfriends in other countries, keeping in contact with people one meets from abroad);

   encouraging the development of appropriate global citizenship values and attitudes in other people *in one's own society* through, for example, supporting cosmopolitan education.

3. Involvement in formal and informal networks. For instance:

non-governmental organisations (NGOs), national or international (which themselves engage in many kinds of activities like political lobbying, education, fostering cultural exchanges, civil disobedience);

working for interfaith dialogue and the development of a global ethic of mutual tolerance;

working within peace organisations such as the Fellowship of Reconciliation;

working within organisations devoted to promoting conceptions of development and environmental responsibility that are seen as conductive to peace.

4. Political lobbying and joining political parties with a view to advancing international peace agendas.

This is a brief indication of the range of expression global citizenship can take. Several aspects are discussed more fully below. These examples illustrate a number of general points. Activities like keeping up with a penfriend from abroad illustrate a feature of many appropriate actions: the developing of such links throughout the world is generally conducive to peace but it is hardly the reason why people do what they do. For it to count as global citizenship, it would have to be either an additional reason that one is contributing to 'a more peaceful world' or, as a by-product, it would have to be one that was welcomed or would be welcomed if the person thought about it. Perhaps at the latter point we would have to say that the 'activeness' of global citizenship had all but gone. But it illustrates the additional point that there are *degrees* of active global citizenship.

Working towards an agreed global ethic or for adequate conceptions of development and environmental responsibility are not, as such, focused on peace but on other global goals that constitute the conditions of peace: peace is the goal but under various guises. The activities under 1 above directed to peace within a country, including interfaith dialogue, are relevant to global citizenship because they parallel what needs to be developed in global attitudes, they facilitate that development, and because, other things being equal, they contribute to global peace by being 'part' of global peace, which is partly constituted by local peace or rather many local peaces. Finally, it is worth remarking that only one of the above activities actually works *through the concept of global citizenship* – namely the promotion of cosmopolitan education in schools. All the activities may be done by people who think of themselves as world citizens but most do not make it their explicit goal.

PEACE ACTIVISM

Activism in the nuclear era

The era of nuclear weapons was ushered in, as almost everyone knows, in August 1945 when two very small atomic bombs were dropped on Hiroshima and Nagasaki, thus bringing to an end the war with Japan. At the time, the USA alone had the bomb but within a very few years the UK, France and the USSR had it, much more powerful 'hydrogen' bombs were developed, and by the beginning of the 1950s, the Cold War had set in and continued until 1989 when it ended with the collapse of the Soviet Union. The possession of massive arsenals of nuclear weapons – capable of destroying the whole world several times over if all were used – was claimed by defenders of it to maintain a kind of 'peace' through the policy of deterrence or mutually assured destruction (MAD): neither side would ever strike first because it knew that the other side could and would strike back. The ethics or rationality of nuclear deterrence, however, is not our concern here (see for example, Lackey 1989; Dower 1998); what is, are the responses to these policies.

Apart from the fact that nuclear deterrence did not prevent many international and civil wars throughout the rest of the world, very large numbers of people were not convinced that there was no real danger of actual nuclear war occurring, and during the Cold War large-scale 'peace' movements mobilised, such as the European Nuclear Disarmament movement (END) and the British-based Campaign for Nuclear Disarmament (CND). These had particularly strong support in the 1960s (when the Cuban missile crisis of 1962 brought the world to the nuclear brink) and the 1980s (when the war was again very cold in terms of East–West hostility).

One particular example is worth mentioning, namely the Greenham Common Women's Peace Camp of the 1980s, in which women protested against the US air base in the UK and the Cruise missiles it was to house. This, amongst many others forms of protest, was significant because it had immense symbolic power in the international peace movements; it represented the importance of non-violent civil disobedience and also the increasing voice of women. As Hutchings points out, it symbolised a new way of thinking about what matters in the world, called, after Ruddick, maternal thinking and a distinctive way of thinking about global citizenship and the kind of ethic underlying it – an ethic of caring and personal relatedness (Hutchings 2002).

The World Court Project

Although tensions eased after the end of the Cold War, many of the weapons remain in place. Indeed, many would argue that the world has become an altogether more dangerous place in terms of the risk of nuclear weapons being used. Many more states have become or are believed to be becoming nuclear states (such as China, Israel, India, Pakistan, Iran and Iraq). A multi-polar world of many oppositions is inherently more unstable than a bi-polar world with a single opposition between NATO and the Warsaw Pact countries during the Cold War. Whilst many groups of activists continue to protest against nuclear weapons in many ways, I will focus on one development, both because of its international character and because it illustrates well global citizenship activism.

In 1987 a group of lawyers led by Sean MacBride issued a Lawyers Appeal calling for the prohibition of nuclear weapons and declared that

> The use, for whatever reasons, of a nuclear weapon would constitute
> (a) a violation of international law;
> (b) a violation of human rights;
> (c) a crime against humanity.

In the same year, Harold Evans, a retired district judge from Christchurch, New Zealand, wrote an open letter to the prime ministers of New Zealand and Australia asking them to take an initiative that would lead to an advisory opinion being sought on 'the legality (or otherwise) of nuclear weapons in international law'. Although this did not get anywhere initially, it was the birth of the World Court Project. In the next few years, many people from many organisations – but especially two professional groups, the International Physicians for the Prevention of Nuclear War (IPPNW) and the International Association of Lawyers Against Nuclear Arms (IALANA) – mobilised public opinion worldwide in order to get the World Court in the Hague to give an 'advisory opinion' on the issue. The issue first went to the World Health Assembly in 1993, which then passed it on to the UN General Assembly. The latter in 1994 asked the World Court to give an advisory opinion, which it gave in July 1996. (See for example, Mothersson 1992; World Court Project 2002.)

Before turning to that opinion, we need to highlight a very important part of the process that led to the matter going to the WHA and the UN. At the beginning of the 1990s, public opinion was mobilised through the circulation of a petition leaflet in which ordinary people were encouraged to sign 'declarations of public conscience' addressed to the World Court. As early as 1907, the de Martens clause of the World Court indicated that the World Court should take into account 'the dictates of the public conscience'. The leaflet, whilst including some facts (for example, that weapons that cause excessive suffering, kill civilians, damage the environment and use poison are already being banned in international law and that the use of nuclear weapons does all of these things), also includes the following declaration:

I affirm:

1. My right to life, a fundamental human right which I believe is threatened by the existence of nuclear weapons.

2. My legal duty, under the Nuremberg Principles, to uphold international law and to act when I believe it is being broken by individuals or governments.

   I believe that the development and deployment of nuclear weapons and the threat to use them are subject to law and may be forbidden by law.

   I therefore call upon all members of the United Nations or other competent organisations to ask the World Court to pronounce upon the legality of nuclear weapons.

The Advisory Opinion of 8 July 1996 included the following crucial clauses:

E. By seven votes to seven, by the President's casting vote, It follows from the above-mentioned requirements that the threat or use of nuclear weapons would generally be contrary to the rules of international law applicable in armed conflict, and in particular the principles and rules of humanitarian law;

However, in view of the current state of international law, and of the elements of fact at its disposal, the Court cannot conclude definitively whether the threat or use of nuclear weapons would be lawful or unlawful in an extreme circumstance of self-defence, in which the very survival of a State would be at stake;

F. Unanimously, There exists an obligation to pursue in good faith and bring to a conclusion negotiations leading to nuclear disarmament in all its aspects under strict and effective international control. (World Court 1996)

Peace movements claimed this as a victory for their cause but the second paragraph of E has been used by the nuclear powers to justify their position. In any case, the opinion constitutes a significant step forward in building up pressure to engage in nuclear disarmament and the peace movements of the world have been encouraged by it. Indeed, appeal to it has been made in national courts in defence of protesters' acts of civil disobedience of domestic law. The World Court Project continues to function. It now defines itself as:

The World Court Project is an international citizens' network which is working to publicise and have implemented the 8 July 1996 Advisory Opinion of the International Court of Justice which could find no lawful circumstance for the threat or use of nuclear weapons. The World Court Project is part of Abolition 2000, A Global Network to Abolish Nuclear Weapons. (World Court Project 2002)

Relevance to global citizenship

At the most basic 'ethical' level of global citizenship, it is clearly premised on a global ethic and an ethic of personal responsibility. Human life and health are universal human goods that are threatened by nuclear weapons. Those involved, if only in signing the declaration, acted as globally responsible agents and encouraged others to do likewise. Grassroots activism, as well as the role of professionals, were well evidenced. Institutionally, a number of dimensions are illustrated. Participation in a complex international coalition of concerned organisations illustrated the political dimension of participation in global governance. It combined the active assertion of a legally recognised right to life believed threatened and the active execution of what is seen as a *legal* duty to uphold international law. An international legal framework is invoked. Indeed, the whole assumption behind it is that progress towards peace and other global values is best achieved through the strengthening of international law, and the world is conceptualised as one legal community. Since citizenship is at least partly constituted by membership of a legal community, it implicitly asserts membership as global citizens of a global legal community.

However, there are many who, whilst also having concerns about peace and perhaps regarding themselves as global citizens, reject or rejected the whole approach of the World Court Project. For those who shared the objective of nuclear disarmament, there were two problems. First, it was a high-risk strategy: what if the World Court had not pronounced as it did? Would that have been helpful? Indeed, in its crucial clause E it came perilously near not accepting it, and in any case the proviso is seen by many pro-nuclear thinkers as letting nuclear powers off the hook. Second, it was irrelevant anyway, since it overemphasised the importance of international law in creating the conditions of peace: other levels and kinds of activity are more important. This reaction might come from both some conventional international-relations thinkers who see nuclear disarmament as a step toward peace being more likely to be achieved by diplomacy, appeals to mutual long-term interests and so on; and also from some in the peace movement itself for whom the cultivation of non-violence at grassroots levels is really what will turn the world around in the long-term. For those who do not share the objective of nuclear disarmament as the crucial means to peace, clearly the whole approach is based on a mistake: such peace as the world can attain depends on armaments and that includes the possession of nuclear weapons by some countries.

My point here is not to agree with any of these criticisms (in fact, I do not) but to show that global citizens need not and do not agree about what forms of activism to engage in. There may be disagreement about the means to be employed, about how to understand the ends pursued and about what is a realistically achievable goal, though all want peace as a value. Though, in practice, relatively few people would say they were global citizens if they supported nuclear deterrence or NATO polices, there is no reason in principle why they should not. Not all global citizens sing from the same songbook. This point is reinforced by the following more specific example of peace activism.

Trident Ploughshares

Trident Ploughshares, invoking the ancient biblical idea of turning swords into ploughshares, is a part of the international nuclear disarmament movement. The UK section of the movement has been active since the mid-1990s and has pledged to 'disarm the UK Trident nuclear weapons system in a non-violent, open, peaceful, safe and fully accountable manner'. 'Trident Plough-share 2000', launched internationally in May 1998, 'aims to train and enable hundreds of international *global citizens* [my italics] to dismantle the British Trident nuclear weapon system'. It does this through acts of civil disobedience, such as illegal entry into submarine bases and related installations, with a view to damaging or destroying equipment. The website contains a catalogue of such actions, subsequent prosecutions and an ensuing mixture of sentences and acquittals (Trident Ploughshares 2002).

One particular case is illustrative (and I mention it not because of its special importance but because I happen to know people involved in it). In June 1999, three women using a dinghy went into Loch Goil, Scotland, entered an unmanned floating laboratory used for testing nuclear submarines and destroyed a large amount of testing equipment estimated to be £100,000 in value. The case was brought before the Sheriff court in Greenock in October 1999. The defendants were acquitted by Sheriff Margaret Gimblett on the grounds that the women were justified in what they had done on the basis of Trident's illegality under international law, specifically the World Court opinion. (This legal decision was challenged in the Edinburgh High Court in November and December 2000 and thrown out in a judgement that attempted to square nuclear deterrence with the World Court opinion.)

My main reason for adding this footnote to the World Court Project is not to commend it. (Indeed, in this case I have reservations about it, both because of the assumed sharp distinction between non-violence toward persons and violence towards property and because some forms of civil disobedience can be counter-productive.) I mention it precisely to reinforce a key point: that what people do in the name of global citizenship may be unacceptable to others but still be clearly a case of global citizen action and be accepted as such by them. It is not merely that what others do may involve ineffective or counter-productive means, or that what they are aiming at may be different, but that the means employed may be, from the thinker's point of view, ethically unacceptable.

THE PROMOTION OF PEACE

I shall discuss other aspects of the promotion of peace under three headings: attitudes towards foreign policy and international relations; elements of cosmopolitan education; and a multi-cultural world.

Foreign policy

There are at least three dimensions to foreign policy that are relevant in examining the possible attitudes and activities of global citizens concerned with peace: first, a country's armaments policy; second, its particular responses to particular conflicts; and third, the general tenor of its foreign policy in regard to promoting or undermining the conditions of peace in the world as a whole.

Thus, (a) a global citizen may work for nuclear disarmament by political campaigning, supporting the World Court Project, going on demonstrations and vigils, or engaging in civil disobedience. (b) A person may be opposed to a particular military conflict, as many were in the UK over the war in the Gulf in 1991 or Kosovo in 1999, or the 'war against terrorism' through the military action in Afghanistan in 2001, and take various forms of action in response. (c) Again, someone may work against the prevailing tendency to 'demonise' the enemy in times of war (or during the Cold War), or the tendency to polarise the world into friends and enemies, like the view of Islam as the enemy of the liberal West (Huntington 1996), and promote the view that Islamic countries and cultures should not be tarred with the brush of a Western perception of 'militant Islam'. (This is particularly pertinent at the current time in the aftermath of September 11th.) (d) If someone thinks that North–South inequalities or the dynamics of modern materialist development are among the background causes of conflict, then she may campaign for changes of attitude in foreign policy (and in public attitudes more generally) *partly* for the sake of peace – though of course for many other reasons as well.

Other global citizens may not accept these forms of action as necessarily right or appropriate. (a) They may take different approaches to nuclear disarmament, as I discussed in the previous section. (b) They may think that the Gulf War and its mode of operation was justified as contributing to the containment of dictatorships and the development of peace conditions in the long run, or that international terrorism will only be stopped or reduced by such military responses. (c) Someone may read geopolitical facts of the Middle East differently: the Islamic threat is inevitable and therefore needs to be confronted and not avoided in a soft liberal or multi-culturalist compromise. (d) North–South inequalities may not be seen as a cause of conflict *as such* (though extreme poverty would need to be tackled) and economic growth may be seen, to adapt an early insight of Kant about the positive connection between economic relations and peace, as the engine of prosperity that, in turn, is the condition of peace.

All these points of view could be adopted by people who would in effect, if not by self-description, be active global citizens, provided they act with a concern for peace in the world as a whole and operate through a variety of institutions with a view to influencing things. Whilst obviously, from any particular point of view, certain forms of action will be better than others – both in terms of appropriate means and in terms of the kinds of goals pursued (linked to different conceptions of peace) – it is better overall if more people are actively concerned about peace at a global level (whatever their views) than if fewer people are (see Chapter 9).

We can, however, despite this fluidity of what is or is not endorsed by global citizens, indicate broadly what approaches to war and peace are inconsistent with *any* global citizenship approach.

First, someone who advocated a 'realist' view of international relations or foreign policy (see Chapter 7) would regard 'ethics' as irrelevant to such considerations: foreign policy is shaped by strategic interests, and although peace as the absence of war may often be preferable from the point of view of national interests, war may sometimes be seen as expedient and 'the continuation of politics by other means' (von Clausewitz 1968: ch. 1). Since global ethics is irrelevant, global citizenship is too. This requires global citizens to be generally opposed to such an understanding of international relations and to be disposed to argue to the contrary if someone adopts it. Taking up the cause of a global ethic against criticism is certainly an active form of engagement!

Second, on the 'internationalist' view, even if one thinks that moral norms do and should determine the behaviour of states, the role of individuals is largely irrelevant to such matters, since the 'morality of states' operates at the level of agreements amongst states. The pursuit of peace is a matter for state-level negotiation and diplomacy, not something for citizens to get involved in. Again, global citizens, or at least those who believe that global citizenship includes active engagement at the global level, have reason to oppose a view that gives them no role. (This characterisation of the 'internationalist' view needs qualification: see Chapter 7.)

Third, whatever theories one might have about international relations, someone might have a general pessimism about human nature as selfish and about the fragility of the human condition that renders working for peace as a 'global goal' a futile exercise. Global citizenship requires a degree of optimism about the possibility of progress, which may simply be denied.

Cosmopolitan education

In her chapter entitled 'Patriotism and Cosmopolitanism' (see Chapter 2), Martha Nussbaum defends the need for cosmopolitan education. Assuming the position of ethical cosmopolitanism of the Stoics, she then asks why teaching children to think of themselves as global citizens is important (see Chapter 8 for criticism). She offers four reasons (Nussbaum 1996):

> First, 'Through cosmopolitan education, we learn more about ourselves', since if we really know about the world, we and our children distinguish what is central to human life and what is accidental to their way of life;

> Second, 'We make headway solving problems that require international co-operation', such as population problems and environmental problems;

> Third, 'We recognise moral obligations to the rest of the world that are real and that otherwise would go unrecognised', especially our duties to tackle world poverty;

> Fourth, 'We make a consistent and coherent argument based on distinctions we are prepared to defend', in that it is only on the basis of genuinely global values that we can find a principled basis for genuine respect in a multicultural society.

Whilst her primary concern was not with peace as such, the case for educating children and ourselves in cosmopolitan knowledge, belief and attitude is entirely applicable to peace education. We need to recognise the importance of being globally educated.

First, whatever else is necessary, such as appropriate attitudes and moral commitments, we need to understand the world. We need to know *facts* about the world – knowledge of other cultures, the realities of aid, global interdependence, the role of transnational companies, the causes of conflict, how the UN works and so on. It is not enough to know about the world in an abstract way. Detailed knowledge of other cultures is important, both because the knowledge is practically important and because in knowing how other people live one can understand oneself better. Furthermore, understanding the world includes understanding the dynamics of war and peace (for example, through 'peace studies'), and the deeper meanings of peace (such as the contrast between positive and negative conceptions mentioned earlier).

Second, although some dispute this way of thinking about ethics, it is important that one explicitly acknowledges the global dimension to ethics. It then becomes clear that one's interest in peace is properly ethical, and that it is based on a concern for the value of peace for anyone in the world, not just for oneself or one's own country. If one took the latter view, one's interest in the conditions of peace would turn out to be largely, if not wholly, prudential or self-interested. Hare once usefully argued that an ethical theory based on the primacy of individual human interests could avoid the dangers of nationalism (putting the interests of people in one's own nation first) and fanaticism (setting up abstract ideals as more important than the interests of people) (Hare 1972).

A global ethic stressing the importance of a common core of values, the equal status of all human beings and the idea of global responsibility underlines the importance of global peace. If local peace is valuable to people in particular places, local peace anywhere is equally important to others and therefore global peace is an object of endeavour. Not all global ethics, however, have this emphasis. A global ethic with a dogmatic proselytising agenda might well not be as good a basis for the promotion of peace.

Respect for difference in a multi-cultural world

This is linked to broader themes already mentioned – knowledge of the world, global values and an understanding of peace itself – but is worth singling out because of its importance and controversial character. Hans Küng once argued: 'there will be no peace in the world without peace among the religions; there will be no peace among the religions without dialogue between them' (Küng 1991; Küng 2002). Differences in religious faith are not, of course, the only source of conflict between different cultural groups but they are a potential source of conflict and illustrate the challenge raised. The challenge is to see how to get those within different cultural groups to engage in dialogue rather than confrontation and to recognise that common values, such as peace, are better served this way than otherwise. Part of Hans Küng's 'world ethics project', based on the Centre in Tübingen, is to create explicit acceptance of what he sees as the essential commonalities (as opposed to less important differences) between the ethical values of the major religions. This is what motivated the *Declaration toward a Global Ethic* of the Parliament of the World's Religions (see Chapter 2).

One aspect of this is the recognition that, whilst it is reasonable to seek a common core of mutually acceptable values, it is not reasonable to expect those with different worldviews – religious or philosophical – to accept one's own worldview. Thus, we may seek a common global ethic as a set of shared values, whilst accepting a diversity of global ethics as theories or 'source stories' (Dower 1998). Another aspect of this is the acceptance of diversity in many of the actual values and norms in different cultures. This is consistent with the kind of global ethic I have suggested informs the thinking of many global citizens. This global ethic accepts a common core of values and norms but also allows for great variation, both in local expressions of these values and in what *further* values and norms are particular to cultures.

Clearly, a middle way needs to be found between a traditional confronting of all beliefs and practices that are at all different from one's own and a relativistic toleration of everything. Few people will try and accommodate those who preach racism, strident nationalism or fanaticism. It is a matter – a difficult matter – of determining where to draw the line between mutual acceptance of diversity, both as a positive value and as a basis of peace and co-operation, and the need, in terms of one's moral values and religious beliefs, to confront beliefs and practices that lie beyond the pale of the reasonable (see also Chapter 8).

Concluding remark

We have seen how much variety there is in the ways people committed to peace worldwide understand peace and promote it. It may seem strange that in a chapter on peace, I have said little about pacifism as a moral principle accepted by individuals not to use killing force in any circumstances. Clearly, much peace activism is inspired by such a view and a belief that the way of peace, dialogue and reconciliation is not merely preferable but morally imperative, since the use of force is wrong. Much peace activism is, however, not based on pacifist assumptions, since for others there may be limited circumstances in which resorting to war is justified. Almost all peace activists can agree that peace as a core human value is often threatened or undermined by the military policies of governments and that a commitment to peace-making, peace-keeping and peace-building are practically important. If my analysis is right, the way of peace and dialogue is to be preferred in all or almost all circumstances, and being a global citizen involves accepting that presumption and acting on it in the various ways I have outlined above.

QUESTIONS

1. How would you define peace? Why is peace important?
2. Is concern for peace a significant part of being a global citizen?
3. If one is committed to peace, what are the most important things to do?
4. Why are some global ethics conducive to peace and others not conducive to peace?

6. DEVELOPMENT AND THE ENVIRONMENT

SUMMARY OF KEY POINTS COVERED IN THIS CHAPTER

The situation
    1.3 billion absolute poor
    Damage to a finite planet
Ethical basis for poverty alleviation
    Poverty as a multi-dimensional evil
    Our duty not to cause it, to aid and to protect
The value of the environment
    Anthropocentrism
    Biocentrism
Sustainable development: fusion of development and environment values
    Critique of international relations and global economy
    Personal lifestyle engagement: beyond immediate benevolence and non-malevolence
Earth Charter
    Publicly shared global ethic
    Appeal to wide range of but not all ethical views
    Integration of full range of human values
Political engagement
    World Development Movement: national grassroots campaigning
    Jubilee 2000: widespread coalition to address debt crisis
Engagement in 'service' organisations
    Médecins Sans Frontières: sacrifice in conflict
    Peace Corps: government-sponsored tapping of idealism
    Environmental Investigation Agency: exposing international crime
    Chipko movement: asserting rights through non-violent action
    Oxfam: curriculum for global citizenship

Introduction

The subject matter of this chapter – aid, poverty, development and the environment – illustrates well the multi-faceted nature of global citizenship. First, we look at the various ethical approaches likely to be taken by those advocating global citizenship – the ethical bases for tackling poverty, thinking about genuine human development and protecting the environment. Second, we look at examples of various forms of engagement by active global citizens, some primarily political and some not so political. We should note in passing that environmentalism has given rise to its own extensions of citizenship, such as environmental citizenship, ecological citizenship and planetary citizenship. These may or may not complement global citizenship, though clearly planetary citizenship comes closest (Thompson 2001).

World poverty

The two most significant factors about the world that have elicited the responses of concerned individuals in the last thirty years – many of whom see themselves as global citizens in so responding – are world poverty and the destruction of the environment. In the mid-1970s, when much active concern developed around these issues, it was estimated that 800 million people lived in 'absolute poverty', a condition described at the time as a condition of life 'so limited by malnutrition, illiteracy, disease, high infant mortality and low life expectancy as to be beneath any rational definition of human decency' (Macnamara 1980). Despite great efforts by the international community, and despite two further decades of development programmes, the situation in the mid-1990s was, in many ways, worse. The Commission on Global Governance states:

> The number of absolute poor, the truly destitute, was estimated by the World Bank at 1.3 billion in 1993, and is probably still rising. One fifth of the world lives in countries, mainly in Africa and Latin America, where living standards actually fell in the 80s. Several indicators of aggregate poverty – 1.5 billion lack access to safe water and 2 billion lack safe sanitation; more than 1 billion are illiterate, including half of all rural women – are no less chilling than a quarter-century ago. The conditions of this 20 per cent of humanity – and of millions of others close to this perilous state – should be a matter of overriding priority. (CGG 1995: 139)

The environmental crisis

In 1972, the first large international conference on the environment took place in Stockholm, thereby signalling widespread recognition of the damage human practices were causing to the natural environment. Serious concerns about the environment, however, largely remained the province of NGOs until the mid-1980s when the Brundtland Report *Our Common Future* (WCED 1987) put the matter firmly on the agenda of both governments and the business world. The idea of sustainable development as a way forward that combined concerns for development and for the environment was officially taken up (some would say taken over) by governments; further commitment to do something was made at the vast Earth Summit in Rio in 1992. Nevertheless, on all the fronts on which problems of the environment were raised in the 1970s, those problems have persisted or intensified.

These can all be seen as aspects of the finiteness of the planet. (a) The finite non-renewable or non-replaceable resources of the planet being used up or destroyed, including the destruction of species (loss of bio-diversity) and destruction of wilderness and natural habitats. (b) The finite capacity of the world to absorb the effects of human activity without change for the worse, particularly in the form of industrial pollution, CO_2 emissions (leading to global warming), desertification and aridification of land through over-cropping, over-grazing and overuse of fertilisers and pesticides. (c) The finite capacity of the biosphere to produce renewable resources, such as food and timber: even if we were not destroying land or polluting the seas, there is an upper limit to renewable production. So although predictions suggest that world population may well stabilise in the middle of this century, they will at best stabilise at levels significantly higher than at present, therefore creating immense challenges over how to use this finite food-growing capacity in sustainable ways that will meet the basic needs of all in an equitable manner, as well as respecting the natural world.

ETHICAL RESPONSES

The above extremely inadequate survey of the world situation sets the scene for the first main issue: what ethical bases are likely to be used by global citizens? (I say 'likely' because a wide range of global ethics and commitments to pursue them are possible.) This is discussed under three headings: the basic ethic; critique of the way things are; personal responsibility. Active global citizenship usually involves all three: not just an ethical basis for concern for the environment and poverty but also a strong sense that the world is in a bad way, that things ought to be done about it, and a willingness to play one's part.

Poverty and development

Extreme poverty is an evil or a bad condition to be in because, apart from its being life-shortening, it generally involves suffering, insecurity, physical disease and weakness, incapacity, disempowerment and loss of dignity. Various ethical theories will order and rationalise these elements in different ways. Utilitarians like Singer stress the need for the conditions for satisfying desires and avoiding suffering/pain and the frustration of desire (Singer 1972). Kantians like O'Neill stress the need for empowerment of the rational agency and control over one's life that poverty undermines (O'Neill 1989). Neo-Aristotelians like Amartya Sen emphasise a range of human 'capacities' that need to be developed and realised for human flourishing to occur (Sen 1999; Crocker 1991). Basic needs thinking, popular in international circles in the 1970s, emphasised the point that, whatever else a person does with her life, she needs certain conditions – that is, certain things are *necessary* preconditions of a satisfactory life (Penz 1991). This idea of preconditions is also reflected in Rawls' idea of 'primary goods' (liberty, material resources and bases of self-respect) (Rawls 1971) and Shue's conception of basic rights (subsistence, security and basic liberty) (Shue 1996a), which we discussed in Chapter 4 (see also Aiken and LaFollette 1996).

Whatever variations there are in the way extreme poverty is seen as bad, it is recognised by almost everyone that other human beings have certain duties in respect to this. The typical understanding (which a global citizen generally goes beyond and challenges) of who has what kinds of duties is as follows. First, we all have a duty not to cause others to fall into extreme poverty (by stealing from them or undermining the bases of their livelihood). Second, if others fall into great poverty – especially if it is through no fault of their own but through natural disasters or the wrong doing of others – individuals have duties of *immediate* benevolence when problems immediately confront them but otherwise have only limited obligations towards others in their own society and even less in respect to distant poverty (though occasionally responses to overseas charity appeals are appropriate). Governments have extensive duties to respond to poverty and so on in their own countries (through welfare safety mechanisms) but also have limited obligations to respond to distant poverty, though even the 0.7 per cent of GNP target for aid from rich countries agreed in the 1970s is rarely met or even approached. Third, in respect to the duty not to allow others to get into conditions of extreme poverty, again individuals have virtually no responsibility to take or support preventative action either at home or abroad, whilst governments have significant obligations to protect people within their own country and limited obligations to give 'development' assistance as part of overseas aid.

Many global citizens, especially those interested in world poverty, challenge this consensus, arguing for a stronger government commitment to overseas aid and for the view that, as members of the global community, we all have significant obligations to give 'emergency' and 'development' assistance.

Environmental values

A physical environment is that which environs or surrounds a person or group of people, both as something that is out there and as something perceived as significant in various ways. As such, it may be seen as valuable either because it serves human purposes in various ways or because it is seen as having a value independent of human purposes. The majority of human beings, including many self-styled global citizens, adopt the former view. This is called anthropocentrism ('human-centredness'). The anthropocentrist may adopt a more narrowly defined instrumental view of this value in seeing the environment as the provider of resources for human well-being and of the conditions for health. A broader view would include the importance of the environment as an object of appreciation (as our 'home' or *oikos*) and as providing areas of natural beauty in which we can get spiritual, aesthetic or recreational satisfaction. If one adopts the second, non-anthropocentric approach, the natural world is seen as a source of 'inherent' or 'intrinsic' value. There is, however, a wide range of views about how to understand this. The 'stewardship' tradition sees humans as having a special role in nature; we are still pre-eminent but have a duty to care for the rest of creation. Biocentrism ('life-centredness') goes further and posits all life as inherently valuable or 'morally considerable', with humans having no special superior status, whilst ecocentrism or environmental holism sees value not just in individual living things but in whole ecosystems (see for example, Attfield 1983; Rolston 1988; des Jardins 1997).

It is beyond the scope of this book to explore these issues in more depth. All we need to note here is that, given that humans generally recognise that certain kinds of environment are positively valuable to people (for either anthropocentric and non-anthropocentric reasons), there are duties to not to undermine them, to help restore them when undermined and to protect such environments. These are usually accepted within local and national communities but also in recent years accepted at international level as creating international legal obligations and so on. This stems partly from the recognition that many environmental problems are essentially global and complex: people in all countries contribute toward the problems, environmental problems arise in complex systems and the solutions require international co-operation and 'systems' thinking (Attfield 1999, 2002; Smyth and Blackmore 2002). A further dimension to ethical thought environmental issues have accentuated, though by no means all theorists agree about this, is that, if certain environments are valuable, they will be valuable to human beings (and incidentally other living things) in the distant future as well, so we need to accept as a dimension of duty or responsibility our obligations to future generations.

There is now widespread acceptance that we need to care for the environment. However, from the point of view of global citizens who are environmental activists, typical responses are inadequate and shallow. They are committed to some form of personal involvement and to critiquing what they see as the inadequate responses of governments and others.

Sustainable development

If it is accepted that certain kinds of environment are bad for anyone and that certain life-conditions are specifically bad for very poor people, and that others, locally, nationally, internationally and globally, have certain kinds of responsibilities to make these bad conditions less frequent, it is important that the two sets of concerns are integrated. Historically, there has been much conflict between environmentalists who wanted to conserve the environment for the well-off and developmentalists who were concerned with social justice for the poor. So the task is to integrate these concerns, which a fully developed global ethic requires. Various attempts have been made to do this but the dominant 'solution' has been the idea of 'sustainable development', defined by the Brundtland Report as 'meeting the needs of the present without compromising the ability of future generations to meet their needs' (WCED 1987: 8). It is a very contested concept, in that for governments and industry it has become the basis of continued economic growth with a green tinge (with new technology seen as the engine of greenery), whereas for critics of conventional 'development' thinking, it requires the abandonment of such thinking and more radical ways of thinking of 'sustainability' (see for example, Dobson 1999; Davison 1996).

Adopting a global ethic according to which poverty and harm to the environment are bad and something ought to be done about them, especially by governments and international bodies, is common enough. Active global citizens are not likely to leave it at that, though. For them, what is striking is how far 'we' are failing to address world poverty and adequately protect our common environment. This calls for political critique and/or personal action. It also calls for a more robust formulation of a global ethic that integrates these and other core values and inspires and unites people to take stronger action. The *Earth Charter*, discussed below, may well serve this purpose.

Engagement as critique

Whether one joins in movements or one acts as an individual, one may critically assess what governments, international bodies and economic institutions do, the rules they work by and so on.

Central to many such critiques is economic globalisation understood as the expansion of the global economy according to neo-liberal assumptions. The growth paradigm is seen as inappropriate: true environmental sustainability cannot be achieved by continued economic growth but rather requires a questioning of Western affluence. For others, the alleviation of absolute poverty through growth in the world economy is not rightly seen as 'trickle down', long-term effects of general prosperity but as something that requires active redistributive measures within and between states. Indeed, the general effect of transnational investment is often seen as undermining the poor: the control of patents by big companies, especially in the areas of biotechnology, actually impoverishes poor farmers. For others, the present international system of states, premised on sovereignty and the right to pursue national interests above all else, may itself be seen as part of the problem that needs addressing.

There is no one radical critique. Indeed, there are many critiques, often in conflict with one another over exactly what the problems are and what the solutions should be. We should not suppose that all active global citizens adopt a radical approach. An alternative approach might be that if we are failing collectively over poverty and the environment, it is not because the system of states and the international economic system are at fault but because of other factors like lack of moral commitment, short-sightedness and corruption, and it is these that active global citizens should be active about. This critical ferment of debate between different perspectives is part of what energises global civil society and makes it an emerging force in global affairs.

Engagement as lifestyle commitment

Global civil society would not be like this without the personal moral commitment of concerned agents. Granted that poverty and environmental harms are very bad and that they are extremely widespread, why should I as an individual do anything about them? (This, of course, includes having the energy to devote to the sort of political critique discussed above as well.) Many global citizens would accept the following analysis as a critique of the conventional understanding of how much individuals need to do.

We need to distinguish between the normal requirement of morality accepted by almost anyone and requirements to further the good, which we might call, somewhat stipulatively, the ethics of responsibility. Apart from specific duties like not lying, not stealing or not breaking promises, most people also accept the requirements of immediate benevolence and immediate non-malevolence – the requirement to help others who need help when one is confronted with it and the requirement not actively to do harm to particular others with whom one interacts. Thus, one should not fail to help someone in trouble, one should not deliberately harm another person, one should not gratuitously destroy a bit of the environment. What distinguishes the active global citizen is an acceptance of an ethic of responsibility that takes one well beyond this paradigm in various ways in respect to global goods. (Others may also accept this ethic of responsibility in respect to goods in their own society, without being, as such, global citizens.)

A global citizen may also accept an ethic of more extensive benevolence. She does not merely help those in front of her, she accepts a general responsibility and seeks out appropriate ways of helping, including helping at a distance. She may join, financially support or even work for a charity or NGO committed to helping. One of the underlying thoughts here is the recognition that there is not all that much difference between actively causing a harm and knowingly allowing a harm to occur that one could prevent if one intervened. Some philosophers have denied any ethically significant difference altogether. A particularly famous example of a thinker whose position comes close to this is Peter Singer, who argued in response to a famine in 1971 that, just as no one would walk on by near a pond in which a child was drowning, so we should not fail to respond to prevent deaths we can prevent in poorer countries, since the same principle underlies both cases: 'if it is now in our power to prevent something very bad from happening without thereby sacrificing anything of comparable moral importance, then we ought to do it' (Singer 1972: 130). This robust statement of an ethical basis for aid has generated considerable debate and no doubt overstates what most global citizens interested in world poverty would accept. For instance, as Fishkin once argued, it undermines the special status of personal relations and leave no 'zone of moral indifference' in which agents are free to do what they want with their lives (Fishkin 1985). But it does, albeit in extreme form, represent one feature of much activity – the willingness to make some sacrifices, certainly in financial or material terms or in terms of easy living, for the sake of others. Many with religious beliefs also see themselves as called to lead lives showing great compassion for others and some disregard for the self.

For many global citizens, the ethical basis for extensive activity rather lies in some theory of justice or human rights. The appeal to justice may centre on the idea of social justice underlying a society (including global society) in which all have a reasonable share of a society's wealth (Beitz 1979) or on the idea of justice as the basis of transactions informed by the principle of uncoerced, informed consent. Since the world is one in which there is manifest inequality in access to wealth and one in which much exploitation occurs, either of these bases is a basis for tackling economic injustice. Likewise with human rights: if the right to economic well-being is not met for millions, this 'minimum demand of all humanity on all humanity' (Luban 1985: 209) provides a basis for action. Undoubtedly, what drives the engagement of many world citizens in addressing world poverty is a sense of injustice and hence solidarity with the oppressed. In explaining the motivation behind such responsible engagement, we have to look to a sense of belonging to the same society or community – in this case, the world – that the ideas of global justice and human rights imply.

The above illustrates how responsible agents move beyond the dominance of the immediate in regard to causing good or combating evil. But equally, we can move beyond the dominance of the immediate in regard to not causing harm too. This is particularly shown in environmental issues by the willingness to accept that one's actions may have indirect (and largely unintended) effects on both distant and future peoples. This is reinforced by acceptance of another feature of actions: their significance lies partly in their contribution to cumulative impacts. Many global citizens become acutely conscious of the damaging effects of lifestyles and the background practices (in industry and so on) needed to sustain those lifestyles. The recognition of the indirect causing of harm provides a powerful reason for concerned individuals to change the way they live and to argue for widespread social and political change. This applies as well to poverty and other more specific evils. The rise of interest in 'ethical consumerism' – attractive to many active global citizens – is a manifestation of this. The goods one buys may be sustaining industries that exploit local labour (trainers and carpets come to mind), produce armaments, tobacco and so on. So if one can find goods that are 'ethically' produced, that is to be preferred (Ethical Consumer 2002). The Fair Trade movement is a manifestation of this. Likewise, 'ethical investment' of one's money in companies or funds that invest in companies that have a good ethical track record is increasing. Although what people do as consumers or investors is often seen as contrasted to what people do as citizens, in this context, given the overarching goal, there is no reason not to think of it as a dimension of being a responsible global citizen.

The Earth Charter

In 1987 the United Nations World Commission on Environment and Development in its seminal Report *Our Common Future* called for the creation of a new charter that would set out the fundamental principles for sustainable development. After the Rio Earth Summit of 1992, renewed efforts were made to develop earlier ideas of an *Earth Charter*. An Earth Charter Commission was formed in 1997, with an Earth Charter Secretariat set up at the Earth Council in Costa Rica. After many years of drafting, there was finally an official launching of the *Earth Charter* at the Peace Palace in The Hague on 29 June 2000. The mission of the current initiative is to:

Establish a sound ethical foundation for the emerging global society and to help build a sustainable world based on respect for nature, universal human rights, economic justice and a culture of peace. (Earth Charter 2002)

The four objectives of the initiative are to disseminate the *Earth Charter* to individuals and organisations; to promote the educational use of the *Earth Charter* in schools and so on; to encourage the use, implementation and endorsement of the *Earth Charter* by civil society, business and government at all levels; and to seek endorsement of the *Earth Charter* by the United Nations (Earth Charter 2002).

The reader is invited to read carefully the full Charter (Appendix 2). Here we merely pick out several salient features of it. It contains a Preamble and a concluding Way Forward, with the central part of the Charter divided into four sections containing in total 16 main principles (and many further sub-specifications). The first section, 'Respect and Care for the Community of Life', contains the four leading principles. The *Earth Charter* illustrates well global citizenship themes.

First, it is something that comes out of the UN system (the Rio Summit and so on) but at the same time has had much input from NGOs and individual experts as well, and thus illustrates an important level of emerging global governance.

Second, it is also an instrument through which individuals will be motivated to care for the world. Its chief use will be as a teaching tool. Personal commitment and 'ownership' of it is encouraged by the invitation to endorse it (which can already be done). The Charter emphasises the element of universal responsibility, declaring

> To realise these aspirations, we must decide to live with a sense of universal responsibility, identifying ourselves with the whole Earth community as well as our local communities. We are at once *citizens* of different nations and *of one world* [my italics] in which the local and global are linked.

Third, the Charter is a form of global ethic that, it is hoped, will form the ethical basis of the emerging global civil society. Thus, the global ethic involved is, in a sense, a publicly shared set of values and norms. It is not, of course, universally shared (perhaps such an ideal – if ideal it is – is quite unrealistic) but it is widely shared and can become more widely shared, and publicly so in the sense that human beings recognise one another as sharing the same principles. The Charter, like the *Declaration Toward a Global Ethic* and the *Universal Declaration of Human Rights*, to the extent that it does become adopted, is part of the 'embodiment' of this global ethic – part of what may be called the globalisation of ethics itself.

Fourth, the principles and recommendations for action are not merely bland or a 'lowest common denominator'. Much of what it says is hard-hitting against common assumptions; for instance, we must get rid of nuclear weapons and all weapons that destroy the environment ('Don't they all?' one might ask) and adopt a view of development that is more about 'being more' than 'having more'. Although it is designed to appeal to a wide range of thinkers whose worldviews are quite different (for example, religious and secular; biocentrist and anthropocentrist), it would not be supported by everyone. Fervent nationalists and ardent supporters of development as economic growth would have problems, as would religious fundamentalists.

Fifth, although it is called an Earth Charter, it is not merely concerned with environmental issues but with all major aspects of human well-being – development, justice, democracy, peace and so on. Most global citizens recognise that the global ethic they should support integrates a wide range of human concerns (even if they personally focus on one aspect). 'Sustainable development' attempts this too, though the *Earth Charter* does not talk of this but of 'sustainable way of life' and 'sustainable global society'. The reader might ponder why this language is preferred.

POLITICAL ENGAGEMENT

We now turn to forms of political engagement. This could as easily belong to the next chapter because of the governance aspect of it but also belongs here because of the examples and subject matter.

World Development Movement

Founded in 1970, WDM describes itself as a 'democratic movement of individual supporters, campaigners and local groups'. It is a UK-based NGO whose primary goal is to put pressure on the UK government, other governments and international bodies to pursue the kind of development that genuinely meets the needs of the very poor. 'Justice for the world's poor' is a slogan it has used. It describes itself as

> Campaigning to tackle the underlying causes of poverty. We lobby decision-makers to change the policies that keep people poor. We research and promote positive alternatives. We work alongside people in the developing world who are standing up to injustice. (World Development Movement 2002)

Over 30 years it has engaged in many campaigns. Amongst recent ones has been a campaign, during and before 1994, that resulted in WDM's getting a High Court victory over the UK Government to stop them squandering £234 million of aid on the Pergau Dam in Malaysia. In 1998, WDM led the British part of a globally integrated campaign in which, for the first time, the role of the Internet in providing rapid communication and mobilisation between activists worldwide was very apparent, to expose the rich OECD governments' intentions to secretly sign the Multilateral Agreement on Investment. The MAI would give more power to multinationals by giving them the right to invest in a country once the latter signed up to it (a Hobson's choice, since not signing would leave a country in the economic cold) and thus weaken governments' rights to stand up to them. To date, the MAI has not been formally concluded. WDM had become one of the founding members of Jubilee 2000 campaigning for Third World debt relief and has been one of the leading NGOs participating in the so-called anti-globalisation protests (WDM 2002). Both these cases will be discussed later.

Mention of WDM serves three purposes. First, it is primarily a political organisation campaigning on political issues. It is not a charity, unlike many NGOs working on humanitarian assistance or environment protection. Second, it is an NGO not an INGO! That is, it is a country-based organisation, not an international or transnational one. But activity within a country is as much an exercise of global citizenship as is working through an INGO. This is both because what determines the appropriateness of the role is the public *objective* of the organisation – namely justice for the world's poor – and because, already noted, the process of globalisation has to some extent rendered irrelevant the formal territorial anchorage of an organisation for determining the kind of social space it really occupies. Third, it is essentially a grassroots organisation: the main activities are conducted by local branches in which volunteer members or supporters do anything from the occasional coffee morning or leafleting to week-in-week-out campaign-related work.

Jubilee 2000

During the 1990s, increasing public concern was expressed about the growing debt burden of most Third World countries. The origins of the debt crisis go back to the late 1970s, when banks were encouraged to lend money generated by the increase in oil revenues but in fact most of the continuing debts have been incurred since by Third World governments borrowing more from rich countries or international lending institutions like the IMF and the World Bank. Often the money borrowed was spent on inappropriate projects or at least on ones that did not benefit the very poor. But that aside, the key problem was the increasing burden of poor countries having to service the debts. Just servicing these debts creates acute financial problems, thus weakening the development efforts of poor countries, so that very poor people, who neither took out the loans nor generally benefited from them, have borne the brunt of reduced public services in health, education and so on. Particularly ironic is the fact that, in many cases, the amount of debt-servicing exceeds the official aid from the countries and international bodies making aid grants.

Jubilee 2000 was a loose coalition of many organisations worldwide campaigning from the middle of the 1990s for debt relief for the most indebted countries. The idea was taken from the 'jubilee' year in the Old Testament (every 50 years) when all debts were cancelled as a way of restoring a level playing field. The hope was that the millennium would provide a moment when rich governments would make a dramatically generous gesture. Mass rallies occurred in many places, most notably in Birmingham in 1998 and Cologne in 1999 to coincide with meetings of Heads of Governments. Some successes were achieved. There is little doubt that under pressure of public opinion, some debt cancellation did occur. For instance, in 1999 the IMF announced proposals to link debt relief to poverty reduction and Gordon Brown, the UK Chancellor of the Exchequer, gave a commitment to cancel up to 100 per cent of poorest country debts to Britain (WDM 2002). The campaign continues now under new labels such as 'Jubilee+' (Jubilee 2000 UK, 2002).

I have singled out Jubilee 2000 because in recent years it has been the most influential of grassroots campaigns mobilising very large numbers of people from many countries. There was a clear global goal, passionate commitment to justice for the poor, extensive networking in formal and informal ways and a clear attempt to influence global governance. Moreover, whilst many involved were from politically oriented institutions like WDM, a very large number were not and were from churches and charities, many but not all of whom were simply responding to what they saw as the manifest and unnecessary suffering caused by the debt crisis. It is significant that the idea of 'jubilee' is the idea of adjustment within a *society*, so applied to the world it suggests the idea of a global society, at least in a moral sense.

OTHER FORMS OF ENGAGEMENT

Médecins Sans Frontières

Médecins Sans Frontières (MSF) is an international humanitarian aid organisation that provides emergency medical assistance to populations in danger. It has set up emergency medical aid missions around the world since 1971 and now operates in more than 80 countries. Whilst its main aim is humanitarian assistance, particularly where health and health systems are at risk, it also seeks to raise awareness of crisis situations. Thus, 'it acts as a witness and will speak out, either in private or in public, about the plight of populations in danger for whom MSF works' (Médecins Sans Frontières 2002).

Although much of its work is in remote areas, its willingness to intervene where the provision of health is disrupted inevitably brings it into war zones. Its work highlights what is increasingly recognised as an important dimension of relief agency work, namely working in situations of military conflict, and thus creating many dilemmas as well as dangers for humanitarian workers (Slim 1998). If citizenship is about willingness to make sacrifices for a greater good, this kind of work illustrates such willingness at a global citizenship level.

MSF's willingness to speak out when its field workers encounter any violation of human rights also illustrates how the work of humanitarian organisations often spills over into political engagement with governments. Whilst some international humanitarian agencies attempt to maintain a strict neutrality to the point of not being drawn into political critique (a notable example being the International Red Cross), many others find it impossible to separate the humanitarian dimension of their work from the political context in which it occurs. Whilst this may raise problems about such organisations being 'charities' in term of the domestic laws of states (with advantages of tax-exempt status), the move from humanitarian work to political involvement is natural enough from the perspective of global citizenship, in so far as citizenship is a political concept. (This is not to suggest that global citizens who see their commitment as purely non-political are somehow unsatisfactory, since the idea has, as we have seen, great fluidity.)

The Peace Corps

The American Peace Corps was set up in 1961. It trains young Americans to go and work in many different countries (around 135), usually for a period of two years; remuneration is low and it is not generally seen as a first step in a career but rather an opportunity for people with idealism to serve others elsewhere before pursuing other careers. Its official aims are:

> To help the people of interested countries in meeting their need for trained men and women;
> To help promote a better understanding of Americans on the part of the peoples served;
> To help promote a better understanding of other peoples on the part of Americans. (Peace Corps 2002)

I mention this example for two main reasons. First, the Peace Corps is not, in the normal sense at least, an NGO, since it is supported by and funded by the American government. Critics may say that, as such, it is really a wing of American foreign policy in promoting American values in the world – even its aims above partly acknowledges this. How far this is so and how far this can be combined with its genuinely having other global goals (such as the good done by the volunteers) are complex issues and lead to wider critical questions about 'the projection of values' in much global citizenship action (Chapter 8). Second, even if the above criticism has some force, it remains the case that the underlying rationale for the organisation has to be sharply distinguished from the motivation of volunteers, many of whom are inspired by global ideals and see themselves as serving others in the world. Active global citizens do not merely belong to the NGO or informal sectors. Nor is this a point merely about young, enthusiastic, poorly paid volunteers! Active global citizenship may be engaged in in many different ways – by government officials or politicians working within national governments, by career specialists working within UN organisations and, last but not least, by 'corporate global citizens' within business companies with a genuine interest in global responsibility, an aspect of 'corporate social responsibility'.

Environmental Investigation Agency

One of the most important things that NGOs can do is to investigate what is happening in the world and, having found relevant information, for example, about human rights abuses, poor workers conditions or the flouting of environment laws, to expose or embarrass or otherwise influence governments and other bodies to improve their behaviour. We saw that this was a feature of Human Rights Watch and here I add an example of work in the environmental field.

The Environmental Investigation Agency was set up in 1984 to 'investigate, expose and campaign against the illegal trade in wildlife and the destruction of our natural environment'. Its main interest is in exposing international environmental crime such as the illegal trade in wildlife, illegal logging and trading in timber species, and the worldwide trade in ozone-depleting substances. Given that we already have much international environmental law such as CITES (Convention on the International Trading in Endangered Species), illegal activities need to be exposed. However, much damage to the environment – regarded by many as morally wrong – is not yet banned by international (or national) law and one of the things EIA also does is to try to influence the development of international environmental law (EIA 2002).

EIA's work illustrates two aspects of global citizenship. First, in exposing breaches of international law, it is in effect invoking, as the World Court Project did explicitly, the Nuremberg principle – that individuals have a duty to uphold international law. Second, in playing a part in developing international law, it is contributing to an increasingly regular phenomenon – the role of NGOs generally in informing international law. International law is, of course, *formally* inter-state law, made by states agreeing with one another; but *substantively* what goes into those laws is influenced by the expertise given and often now welcomed by those responsible for framing such laws. The presence of NGOs at international conferences, often through informal conferences running parallel, is also evidence of the same phenomenon of interaction – sometimes frictional, sometimes symbiotic – between NGOs and the governmental sector.

The Chipko movement

The Chipko movement started spontaneously in April 1973 when a group of women desperate to stop the logging of the trees that were part of their livelihood stopped the contractors by literally hugging or embracing (chipko) the trees. The success of this led over the next five years to similar events in many districts of the Himalayas in Uttar Pradesh and has since spread further. It now involves hundreds of decentralised and locally autonomous initiatives. Village women are the leaders and main activists and their objective is to save their means of subsistence and their communities. One of the most significant aspects of the movement is its commitment to *satagraha* (truth power) or non-violent resistance – thus expressing in practice an aspect of Gandhi's philosophy. It has been an effective movement, including a major victory in 1980, when a 15-year ban was ordered by the Indian Prime Minister on green felling in the state's Himalayan forests. (The information here is gained from a number of Internet sources.)

My main reason for including this movement is to illustrate an important aspect of global citizenship, namely that its active expression is as much about the assertion of rights as it is about the exercise of responsibility, and to provide an example of activism in poorer countries. As we saw with the example of Greenham Common, where a main driver for the action was not wanting nuclear weapons on one's doorstep, what drives activism may be self-interested and the protection of one's own rights. But it is not just that. These rights are seen as part of a global vision and the actions are seen symbolically as part of a global solidarity with others with like values and challenges (and perceived reciprocally by others too). This illustrates seeing the local in the global and vice versa, or as an example of 'glocalisation' (Robertson 1992; Tomlinson 1999). Furthermore, global citizenship is not just something people from the North (rich countries – stereotypically also white, middle class, highly educated) actively express for the sake of others. Though the amount of activism in poorer countries is, of course, less than in rich countries – and this itself ought to be and is to some extent a matter of concern to NGOs themselves – it is important to remember that it happens. If global citizenship were only for the wealthy elites of rich countries, it would indeed be problematic.

Oxfam and development education

Finally, I mention Oxfam, not because of its extensive overseas development work but because it places importance on development education. If, in the long-term, the prospects of poorer countries are to improve, it depends on changes of priorities in rich countries and their governments and this requires better education about the world and the development of appropriate attitudes in electorates. In fact, Oxfam has developed over the last few years a programme explicitly called the 'Curriculum for Global Citizenship'. I conclude with several excerpts:

Oxfam sees the Global Citizen as someone who:

is aware of the wider world and has a sense of their own role as a world citizen;
respects and values diversity;
is willing to act to make the world a more equitable and sustainable place;
takes responsibility for their actions.

The key elements for responsible Global Citizenship:

Knowledge and understanding
Social justice and equity
Diversity
Globalisation and interdependence
Sustainable development
Peace and conflict

Skills
Critical thinking
Ability to argue effectively
Ability to challenge injustice and inequalities
Respect for people and things
Co-operation and conflict resolution

Values and attitudes
Sense of identity and self-esteem
Empathy
Commitment to social justice and equity
Value and respect for diversity
Concern for the environment and commitment to sustainable development
Belief that people can make a difference (Oxfam 1998)

Whilst it is clear that not all active global citizens would sign up to this exact list or all the values it assumes, it represents a significant checklist of the sorts of things associated with someone being an active global citizen. It is also worth nothing that the implied definition of global citizenship makes no reference to the institutional dimensions I have mentioned and it is a useful reminder that, for many, ethical commitment is the core of the concept. Of course, Oxfam assumes that to be effective in the world one will use NGOs (like Oxfam) and other political opportunities for action. But these institutions are more thought of as the means or instruments of effective action rather than as part of defining character of being a global citizen. Whether this is adequate is the issue for the next chapter.

QUESTIONS

1. What arguments are there for helping to alleviate world poverty?
2. What is valuable about our environment?
3. Would you endorse the Earth Charter? If so, why? If not, why not?
4. Considering the examples given of active engagement in global concerns, do you think of these as examples of global citizenship, and if so, what are the main features?

---

7. THE UNITED NATIONS AND GLOBAL GOVERNANCE

SUMMARY OF KEY POINTS COVERED IN THIS CHAPTER

Global governance
    Through range of institutions including global civil society
    Through the society of states
    Through world government
    Importance for global citizenship
The United Nations
    Brief history
    United Nations Associations
Arguments for supporting the UN
    Symbol of international co-operation
    Embodiment of global citizenship
    Same goals as global citizens
    Responses to conflict
    Development of international law
Arguments for not supporting the UN
    Ineffectiveness and corruption
    Lack of democracy
    Replies
Global civil society
    Is it democratic?
    Is it part of governance?
    Cosmopolitan democracy
World government
    World Federal Movement
    Necessity for peace, justice and enforceable law
    Rejection of this necessity and risk of global tyranny
    World government only desirable when not necessary

INTRODUCTION

Governance is described by the Commission on Global Governance as 'the sum of the many ways individuals and institutions, public and private, manage their common affairs' (CGG 1995: 2). Global governance then is the way we manage our common affairs at the global level. As such, governance is distinguished from government, since government is generally taken to indicate an institution with formal, usually authorised, power to control aspects of people's lives over which government is exercised, generally with the backing of coercion. Government may indeed be and usually is the dominant mode of governance, at least in regard to governance within national states. The question arises: what other forms of governance are possible and desirable? Although our concerns are with the global level, it should be noted that the question is equally pertinent at both sub-state and state levels too, and its perceived importance has been partly triggered by the process of globalisation.

Commission on Global Governance

The particular conception of global governance put forward by the Commission includes the following helpful elements:

At the global level, governance has been viewed primarily as intergovernmental relations, but it must now be understood as also involving non-governmental organisations (NGOs), citizens' movements, multinational corporations, and global capital markets. Interacting with these are global mass media of dramatically enlarged influence. [. . .]

There is no single model or form of global governance, nor is there a single structure or set of structures. It is a broad, dynamic, complex process of interactive decision-making that is constantly evolving and responding to changing circumstances. [. . .]

The creation of adequate governance mechanisms will be complicated because these must be more inclusive and participatory – that is, more democratic – than in the past. [. . .] A multifaceted strategy for global governance is required. This will involve reforming and strengthening the existing system of intergovernmental institutions, and improving its means of collaboration with private and independent groups. It will require the articulation of a collaborative ethic based on the principles of consultation, transparency and accountability. It will foster *global citizenship* [my italics] and work to include poorer, marginalised and alienated segments of national and international society. (CGG 1995: 2–5)

The assumption here is that, given the range and nature of modern world problems, the only way that these can be managed properly is through involvement of and consultation with individuals and various kinds of bodies other than formal government institutions. This involvement is conceived of as democratic, though the idea of democracy is very broadly defined to go beyond formal decision-procedures. International institutions need strengthening and reforming. Here they have in mind primarily the UN and the UN system – but this is not, as they note elsewhere, a prescription for world government, which they oppose.

Whilst I am broadly sympathetic to this way of thinking of global governance, not least because it provides a space into which to insert global citizenship, its conception of global governance is to be contrasted with at least two other ways of thinking about it. This leaves rather open just how global citizenship fits into the picture (see for example, Tomlinson 1999).

Global governance through the society of states

One answer (implied by the opening sentence of the quote above) is that global governance is best delivered by the international society of states. States provide formal coercive government for the populations over which they exercise sovereignty and, more informally, less coercive governance in respect to global matters that need management through co-operation with one another at international level. The maintenance of order and of the conditions necessary for world trade, travel and communications, and increasingly nowadays responding to common environmental problems and problems of world poverty, require co-operation and the development of and compliance to rules, regulations and international laws. But these are all goals that states *and states alone* are responsible for and effective in delivering. In this model there is no space, either as a matter of fact or normatively, for a significant input from global citizens or global civil society. (This internationalist model is criticised at various points later on.)

Global governance through world government

The other form of global governance that conflicts with their conception is one in which global governance is, in fact, equated with or at least premised on world government. Global problems are not going to be managed properly without the coercive regulatory power currently exercised by the nation-sate being transferred to a single global authority. Such a world state might or might not be democratic and it might or might not include a significant role in governance for NGOs, global civil society or engaged activists. Nor is it in itself hostile to the idea of global citizenship. (The arguments for and against world government are assessed at the end of this chapter. The argument for making global citizenship dependent on world government is assessed in Chapter 9.)

The importance of global governance

Why is global governance important for the study of global citizenship? Two kinds of reasons can be given, one instrumentalist and the other conceptual.

First, a global citizen might have certain global goals, engage in action through global civil society and believe others ought to do the same but regard the institutions of governance as based on what governments and international institutions do. As such, these institutions of governance need to be influenced, restrained, guided and so on by *inter alia* the activities of global civil society (including, of course, the press and media exposure). Global citizens use, support or criticise the institutions of governance but are not part of them.

Second, global citizenship may be conceived as being part of global governance. Global citizens, in acting in the ways they do, are participating in global governance, in that they are both influencing global affairs, have a right to do so and ought to be so regarded as having that right by states and the international society of states. This conceptual approach raises several questions. First, is such participation as occurs now to be thought of as democratic or not? Even if it is not, is such action, in the absence of democracy at the global level, to be regarded as a legitimate form of influence in global decision-making? And should we strive for a more effective form of global governance through more formal patterns of 'global democracy' or 'cosmopolitan democracy'?

These issues are explored first through a discussion of the United Nations, which illustrates well many of the different possible relationships global citizenship can have with global governance. Then we look at global civil society, the different ways it can be seen to articulate with global governance and the question whether it is democratic. This leads us to examine a specific proposal for global governance, namely cosmopolitan democracy, and finally an examination of the arguments for and against world government.

THE UNITED NATIONS

Some background facts

The Charter of the United Nations was signed on 26 June 1945 shortly before the end of the Second World War and it came into force on 24 October 1945 – a date subsequently celebrated in many parts of the world as 'UN Day'. The Preamble to the Charter speaks of 'We the Peoples of the United Nations, determined to save succeeding generations from the scourge of war . . . .'.

Although it speaks of 'We the peoples', it is *formally* an inter-state organisa-tion. Its members are nation-states – a fact of some significance for its relevance to global citizenship, as we will see below. It originally had 52 members and gradually, through the rest of the world becoming decolonised and through other developments after the Cold War, it has become enlarged to around 190 member states – virtually the whole world community.

Officially the UN's primary function has been ensuring security and the prevention of military conflicts. But the Charter indicates three other main aims that, over the years, have assumed greater importance: to reaffirm faith in fundamental human rights; to establish conditions under which justice and obligations arising from treaties can be maintained; to promote social pro-gress and better standards of life in larger freedoms.

Its chief organs include: the General Assembly in which all nations, large and small, have seats, each with one vote; the Security Council in which five states (USA, UK, France, Russia (formerly USSR) and China) have permanent seats and the right to exercise the veto (the Security Council being authorised to take action to deal with threats to international security); the Secretariat headed by the Secretary General; various bodies such as ECOSOC (The Economic and Social Council). There are also many other organisations, either specialised agencies or other bodies (some predating the UN) associated with the UN and seen as part of the UN system, such as: WHO (Health), FAO (Food and Agriculture), UNDP (Development Programme), UNEP (Environ-ment Programme), UNESCO (Education, Science and Culture), UNICEF (Children's Fund), the World Bank (which gives loans and grants for devel-opment), IMF (International Monetary Fund, which give loans to countries experiencing financial difficulties, usually with 'conditionalities' attached) and the World Court (which arbitrates in disputes between countries) (see for example, Luard 1979).

The UN is not, however, a world government, though if it had acquired a standing military force, as envisaged in the early days but rendered impossible by the Cold War, it might have become more like a world government, with coercive power to make nations comply to its decisions. In terms of its rationale as an international institution, it was conceived of as a body through which autonomous sovereign states co-operate.

Should a global citizen support the United Nations?

It may seem obvious that anyone who is a global citizen both should and does support the United Nations. After all, as Imber points out in a study that is critical of the UN, the aims of the United Nations are the aims of almost all global citizens – these goals require co-operation between states and the development of international law and the UN exists to facilitate co-operation for these goals (Imber 2002). Nevertheless, many people with a keen commitment to work for a better world, some of whom may think of themselves as global citizens, may reject the UN because it fails to achieve its objectives, because it is the wrong kind of organisation, or because it is irrelevant to the real global transformations needed. Whilst I argue that the criticisms of the UN have to be taken seriously, on balance the case for supporting it is strong, given at least the kinds of global values I accept and believe are accepted by most global citizens. This defence does, however, depend on adopting a position of *critical* support/loyalty midway between uncritical support and unsupportive criticism.

The question of whether global citizens should support the United Nations or not is nonetheless different from the question of whether the United Nations embodies global citizenship or not – that is, whether its existence is a significant part of what *makes* us global citizens (as human rights law, as we saw in Chapter 4, arguably does). Of course, one reason why global citizens should support the UN might be that it does partly constitute their identity, and one reason why someone might not support the UN is because, from her understanding of the UN, the UN does nothing of the kind. But the two sets of attitudes need not go together. The UN might be worthy of support even if it was not the embodiment of global citizenship. There are plenty of other considerations involved.

United Nations Associations and WFUNA

Before giving the reasons for supporting the United Nations, we should note that there is one kind of organisation that has as its explicit goal support for the United Nations. In most countries of the world there are United Nations Associations. These are not all the same, since some are government-sponsored bodes and others, like the UNA-UK, are autonomous bodies, independent of both their national governments and the United Nations itself, that see their role as that of promoting knowledge of and support for the United Nations and for its work in tackling a comprehensive range of global problems. These UNAs are formally linked together into a world federation of UNAs (WFUNA), which, through its ongoing work and international gatherings, provides significant inputs of ideas and proposals from grassroots activists into the UN system.

I mention these organisations because they provide a tangible example of global citizenship, especially if one thinks that some kind of institutional link with world institutions is important to its being *citizenship*. UNAs have both direct and via-WFUNA links to the most significant international body that exists. It is, however, important not to exaggerate this special role or relationship as significant for global citizenship. First, many other organisations and the individuals within them support the United Nations or aspects of its work. (If we measured support for the UN by membership of UNAs, it would be weak indeed.) Second, promoting global goals through NGOs or INGOs need not involve going through the UN or indeed support for the UN. Active global citizenship takes many forms.

Reasons why global citizens should support the UN

Symbolically, the UN is an embodiment of the global moral perspective that goes beyond nationalism and sectional interests. Though theorists in international relations may think of it as a device used selfishly by states to promote their own interests (accepting that generally 'jaw-jaw' is better than 'war-war'), its very structure and mode of operation encourages co-operation and co-ordination and the development of policies that can be justified to all parties affected. It may not always succeed, of course.

Furthermore, the UN's institutions, though they are not institutions of world government, are nevertheless the most obvious manifestation of global governance and provide the analogue at the global level to the institutions of government at the national level. Ordinary people are linked to it via their state's participation in it and get some of the institutional character of their global citizenship from it.

The UN's official goals are very similar to those shared by most global citizens, such as peace and security, human rights, social and economic progress, and protection of the environment. Much of the progress made on these fronts has been facilitated through the UN in various ways. One concrete example of this was the decolonisation process over which the UN presided and that has transformed the world into a world of sovereign states (which it definitely was not in 1945), and linked to this was the UN-co-ordinated pressure against apartheid in South Africa. Thus, global citizens have good reason to support an organisation that furthers their ends.

Over the years, the UN has played its part in containing violent conflict, whether through the often unnoticed 'good offices' of the Secretary General and his colleagues, or through the intervention of peace-keeping forces. Some of the latter operations have been successful but some in recent years have not.

The UN is the forum through which much international law is developed, adopted and ratified. Respect for international law is the cornerstone of the slow progress towards a more civilised world in which there is less reliance on violence and the threat of violence in the pursuit of ends. The UN has also presided over many international conferences, such as the Earth Summit in Rio in 1992, and produced many international declarations and agreements.

Reasons why a global citizen might not support the UN

The criticisms of the UN fall into two categories: first, although the basic institutions of the UN are sound enough, it does not work properly and fails to achieve its objectives; second, its structures are themselves unsatisfactory.

First, as Imber catalogues in considerable detail, the UN has failed to achieve its objectives in many areas – whether this is in the area of containing armed conflicts or providing aid or protecting rights (Imber 2002). There have been almost 300 major conflicts in the world since the UN was set up and active intervention by the UN has often been disastrous (as in Somalia or Bosnia); human rights are only selectively protected and UN aid programmes have often been unsuccessful. The UN and its agencies have been dogged with administrative problems, heavy-handed bureaucracy, corruption and so on. Furthermore, it has been said that the road to global disaster has been paved with many international conferences and, for all the growth of international law, such developments of unenforceable law have little effectiveness in a world dominated by selfish states.

Second, the UN is commonly criticised for being undemocratic. This criticism often centres on the power of the Security Council and the special status of the five permanent members with the veto power, though there is a more general criticism that because the UN is an inter-state organisation it does not and perhaps cannot really reflect the interests of ordinary people or the transnational influences of emerging global civil society. Even if it is a body we need, it is certainly not the right kind of body through which anything like global citizenship could express itself. In any case, alternative forms of governance are emerging in the world that render the UN less central than it was.

Replies to criticisms

That the UN and its organs and agencies have many faults may be granted. But this can be said out of critical loyalty rather than negative criticism, if the possibility of improvements is accepted. At the same time we have to be careful not to judge the UN by unrealistically high standards – a temptation, given that it was set up with high idealism. As Luard once remarked, it is only because people have unrealistic and utopian expectations of the UN that they 'condemn [. . .] inadequacies which elsewhere they would accept as inescapable' (Luard 1979: 3). Furthermore, with regard to all the failures in stopping conflicts, in development programmes and so on, we need to recognise that there are lots of successes as well. More to the point, we need to see that the failures are often the product of a lack of will on the part of states to use the UN properly for its purposes. The internationalist John Ferguson once remarked that if someone says that the UN has failed, one should reply 'I'm glad you admit your failure. Now what are you going to do about it?' (Ferguson 1988: 3). Although 'we the people' have in reality no formal input into the UN, the attitudes of our governments towards the UN (as on many other things) is a function what we their electorates favour or advocate.

For all its faults, the UN is works supporting. The question we have to ask is: would the world be a better place if we did not have an international organisation like the UN and either had none or something very different? The supporter will say that the answer is clearly 'no'. The critic will say 'yes'. Between the supporter and the critic there may be a large measure of *factual* disagreement about success rates, degrees of bureaucratic inefficiency and corruption, the amount of positive outcomes from conferences and the difference having international laws as opposed to not having them makes, and so on. But the disagreement may also turn on more subtle issues about what kind of an organisation the UN is and how order and other values are best maintained in the world.

At one extreme, not occupied by global citizens, there is a realist critique of the UN as being marginal to the real interplay of power in the world and as something to be used for advancing national interests. Global citizens can, in reply, only advance general anti-realist arguments at this point (see Chapter 8).

At the other extreme, perhaps occupied by some global citizens sceptical of the UN, the UN may be criticised as needing to be bypassed because it is an inter-state organisation and there are other, more effective ways of promoting a better world through NGOs, governments acting bilaterally, or informal networking. A UN supporter can reply, even if she recognises the importance of these other ways of promoting global values, that the UN remains an appropriate object of critical loyalty, partly because it symbolises in the most concrete manner available in the world today the idea of international co-operation.

The criticism that the UN is undemocratic raises new issues. Reform of the Security Council is, for many, long overdue but slow progress on this is not reason enough not to support the UN as such. Likewise, the fact that ordinary people do not directly elect representatives to the UN itself or to its bodies does not give one reason not to support the UN but rather reason, if one thinks that it should become democratic in this way, to advocate its becoming more democratic. Indeed, there has been a movement called CAMDUN precisely devoted to this goal – the campaign for a more democratic United Nations (see for example, Archibugi 1995).

Is the UN an embodiment of global citizenship?

But does the fact that the UN is currently not democratic in this way entail that it is not the appropriate embodiment of global citizenship? This does not follow, since there are many other elements to global citizenship and the goal of making the UN more democratic may be seen as an *aspirational* element of current global citizens. Only if one thought that cosmopolitan democracy defined as formal democratic structures at global level was essential to global citizenship, would the UN as it is clearly not be an embodiment of global citizenship. I explore the idea of cosmopolitan democracy further below.

Still, the critic might insist, the UN is not a *global* organisation but an *international* one. It is an inter-state organisation and its rationale is the maintenance of the system of states by first and foremost respecting sovereignty. As such, it is premised on a conception of world order in which the individual has very little role outside each nation-state sphere. It contributes to the model 'order within states and order between states'. It is therefore in conflict with global citizenship, not its embodiment.

There is, however, a paradox at the heart of the UN. Although it is an interstate organisation, it is also premised on global goals such as justice and human rights, which go well beyond the traditional norms of international society. Increasingly, appeals to human rights have been the basis of interventions. Recent interest in the idea of states as 'international citizens' or *good* international citizens represents an attempt to maintain states as the central actors in world affairs whilst legitimising them as really being the standard-bearers of cosmopolitan goals like justice, human rights, poverty reduction and environment protection (Williams 2002; Linklater 1992). Whether or not it really make sense to say that states are *citizens* of the society of states, the addition of this idea does not preclude a parallel conception of global citizens as *individuals* with a role to play and, indeed, invites a partnership with global citizens.

Whilst the UN may have been born in an intellectual environment in which it had a clearly defined role in a clearly defined international system, there is no reason at all why it should not evolve and our thinking about it evolve too, so that it reconstitutes itself in ways that take into account the activities of global civil society and active individuals within it.

GLOBAL CIVIL SOCIETY

We have considered many examples of engagement by active individuals in global civil society – primarily examples of people, active through humanitarian organisations, political pressure groups, churches and more informal networking. We have taken the view that such individuals are, in so acting, acting as active global citizens (especially if they so describe themselves). This may be disputed, both by critics of global citizenship and also by some advocates. For instance, an advocate of global citizenship, van den Anker, takes the view that global citizenship as an institutional conception requires participation in institutions with at least the power to determine formal rules or regulations, so, although we are already moral cosmopolitans, we are not yet institutional cosmopolitans (van den Anker 2002). I consider these critical moves further in Chapter 9 but consider here two key questions: is what agents do within global civil society democratic? is what they do part of global governance? If we think that global civil society does contribute to democratic expression and does form part of global governance, then we not only establish that agents acting within it are by that token members of some form of global *polity* – our current issue – but also a fortiori give an argument for a positive answer to the question for Chapter 9, namely that global civil society does indeed make us global citizens. But the converse does not hold. Even if we concluded that global civil society did not contribute to democratic expression or global governance, it does not follow that agents active in it are *not* global citizens, since we may hold that they are global citizens simply in virtue of other kinds of factors.

Is global civil society democratic?

Clearly, we need to adopt an informal understanding of democracy if we are to see what people do within NGOs and other organisations of global civil society as democratic. Following Scholte's definition given earlier (p. 46), a case can be made for this. This kind of involvement can be called a form of global democracy. McGrew identifies three forms of global democracy: liberal-democratic internationalism, roughly the picture of global governance envisaged by the Commission on Global Governance based on reform of the international community with the support of NGOs; radical communitarianism, which makes more of the emergence of '*alternative* forms of global social, economic and political organisations based generally on communitarian principles', and thus making more of global civil society as constitutive of new forms of democratic governance; and third, cosmopolitan democracy as a proposal for more formal democratic arrangements at global level (discussed below) (McGrew 2000: 407).

In his discussion of globalisation, Scholte raises a possible difficulty about my identifying global citizenship with participation in such networks and associations. He recognises that, in many ways, such phenomena are not democratic. NGOs and the associations of global civil society may not be democratic, both because they represent a very small number of people and because they are themselves often not internally democratic. Global networks (for example, people co-operating through the Internet) are again very unrepresentative, in that on the whole it is rich elites that have access to computers and so on. Likewise, in respect to consumer powers in the market place, he notes that the very poor do not really have any say in the global market place (Scholte 2000).

As I noted above, the idea of global citizenship does not strictly entail 'global democracy' (any more than citizenship itself entails democratic citizenship in a state). However, since most people who act as global citizens *do* see themselves as committed to democratic values and *do* think of what they do as broadly democratic, we need to consider this carefully.

First, in a world where there is a dramatic democratic deficit, we can ask: do the actions of people who promote global causes in various ways contribute toward a world that is more democratic or not? If a world is more democratic because the voices of more people are heard, or heard more effectively, then the engagement of more people in such processes would appear to contribute to this, even though they are not formally representing constituencies in the way that the liberal democratic model might suggest. This raises the question: what would make the world more democratic? Perhaps, as some like Held and Archibugi argue, we should be moving towards more formal democratic structures at a global level that replicate the existing forms of state democracy. Perhaps, given Scholte's rather looser characterisation of democracy, we should be looking to the development of other structures and relationships, as well or instead.

Second, whilst the internal structure of NGOs is indeed of concern in so far as they are not themselves democratic, it has to be said that there is an important difference between an association that is voluntary and something like the political community of the nation-state, which, at least for most of its members, provides a non-voluntary regulatory framework. NGOs flourish in so far as they are supported by contributions, membership subscriptions and, apart from a core of paid employees (who don't have to work for them), usually a large number of unpaid activities. If those involved are prepared to put up with the non-democratic aspects of their association, then that is their choice. This is not an argument for not being concerned about it (democracy and transparency would indeed make such an organisation even more attractive) but it is one for saying that global citizenship may express itself through less than fully democratic associations without embarrassment.

Third, even if global civil society is in reality made up of active agents who constitute only a tiny fraction of the world's population, this does not mean that these agents are not citizens exercising their democratic powers. The fact that active citizenship is something exercised by a small proportion of people is no more an argument against global democracy than it is an argument against national democracy. The fact that few people are actively involved in such networks and associations does not make them undemocratic either. Even within a formally constituted democracy, the influence of activists out of proportion to their numeric strength has to be recognised. A person who joins a political party, who writes a letter to her MP or joins an NGO that lobbies government, is by her action attempting to exercise an influence out of proportion to her fraction of the voting population. This, far from being an undermining of democracy, is part of its essence, at least if the idea of active participation is seen as part of citizenship in a democracy. Likewise, involvement in global activities in order to influence the way decisions are made at other levels is by the same token democratic as well. Of course, it is not formally democratic in the sense that what is done is mandated by all people voting in referenda or authorising representatives in an election. But that sense of democracy is not the only one that is significant and, in the absence of any such formal procedures at the global level, there is good reason to see the activities of NGOs as both expressing and advancing democratic values. This is why the rejection by government spokespersons such as Clare Short (Secretary of State for the Department for International Development of the UK government) of what the so-called 'anti-globalisation' protesters at Genoa in July 2001 were doing as undemocratic was not helpful (BBC Radio 4, 24 July 2001) – nor are such protests (also for example, at Seattle, Washington and Gothenburg) really 'anti-globalisation', since they manifest 'globalisation from below'.

Is global civil society part of global governance?

If what people acting in global civil society do is, in some sense, democratic, then it would seem to follow that it is part of governance, since, whatever a government as a limited body of people do, the democratic framework provides both positive inputs (via electoral preferences) and checks on what governments both do and ought to do. On the other hand, forms of governance need not be democratic. So an interpretation of global civil society as contributing to democracy entails that it is a part of governance. But more needs to be said, both because the entailment might be questioned and because global civil society might be part of global governance without its being seen as democratic.

First, it is not obvious that people acting as citizens in a democratic framework are contributing to governance. If governance is, as Scholte suggests, what provides a regulatory framework, then democracy may provide constraints and inputs and give legitimacy to what those who govern do – but they are not nevertheless governing. In this sense, it would be fanciful to suppose that all ordinary people *could* contribute to governance and an exaggeration to suppose that those active in NGOs and pressure groups are *really* contributing to governance, even though they may significantly influence what rules and regulations those in governance come up with. Global citizenship is in no worse a position in this regard than citizenship itself and failure to be part of governance is not a reason to deny that either citizens or global citizens *are* citizens. But this conclusion depends on a narrow interpretation of governance that limits governance to regulation-setters rather than including those who influence and have a right to influence the regulation-setters. If democracy is partly about self-governance or auto-nomy, then citizens play their part in *governance* (by voting and active engagement), if not in government.

Second, even if global civil society is not seen as democratic, it remains the case that what people do in such organisations does have a significant impact on government policies and on the development of laws. I remarked in Chapter 6 that NGOs may have a significant impact on the groundwork for and formulation of environmental laws, so that although it is states that pass these laws, the substance of them reflects inputs from bodies that are not *formally* part of government qua law-setters but clearly contribute to how we order our public affairs, as the Commission puts it.

Cosmopolitan democracy

Prominent amongst advocates of cosmopolitan democracy have been David Held and Daniele Archibugi. In books like Held's *Democracy and Global Order*, they argue that the processes of globalisation have created the space in which new patterns of democratic engagement can emerge. This is essential if we are to make up the 'democratic deficit' caused by the fact that global forces render national governments unable to deliver on democratic mandates within their own countries (Held 1999). Whilst part of the thrust of their thinking is to endorse the active role of people within global civil society, which as we have seen is a form of informal global democracy, what is distinctive in it is the advocacy of the further development of formal democratic institutions at a transnational level. 'The cosmopolitan model of democracy attempts to specify the principles and the institutional bases upon which democratic governance within, between and across states is to be expanded' (McGrew 2000: 413). Central to that achievement of democratic autonomy is the necessity for a cosmopolitan democratic law that 'transcend[s] the particular claims of states and extends to all in a "universal community" ' (Held 1999: 228) and to which states are subject in a more profound sense than they are subject to international law at present. The development of democracy at the European level within the EU (with the combination of national citizenship and European citizenship) is seen as a beacon of future possibilities. Ideas for a more democratic UN discussed above are amongst the possibilities considered (Archibugi 1995).

Critics such as Axtmann (Axtmann 2002) and Kymlicka (Kymlicka 1999) are quick to point out the problems with these proposals. Apart from questioning how influential global civil society really is and questioning their democratic credentials because of lack of formal representation and account-ability, proposals for more robust and formal democratic institutions at global level are treated with scepticism. This is partly, they claim, because of lack of proper accountability mechanisms but mainly because global goals are better served by maintaining or strengthening the state. This means making the state more democratic and making the international system work more effectively as a system of states rather than introducing this complex, fluid and confusing new layer of governance. Writers like Richard Falk, however, see this fluidity as part of the exciting new developments in global relationships in which new possibilities of governance emerge (Falk 2002).

'Cosmopolitan democracy' makes explicit what 'global democracy' contains implicitly, namely reference to a democracy of global *citizens* (cosmo *polites*). Clearly, if we accept the idea of cosmopolitan democracy, then we are giving an account of global citizenship, and a robust one at that, in that a conception of some kind of global polity is envisaged in which people can exercise their democratic power in some formal way. It represents a kind of halfway house between the kinds of participation in governance open to people acting through currently available institutions and formal membership of a world state. Whilst I have defended a view of global citizenship that does not require the presence of formally democratic institutions at global level, clearly the development of such would strengthen the institutional embodiment of global citizenship. So long as the continued existence of the state system is accepted, as Archibugi argues (Archibugi 1995), alongside new forms of cosmopolitan democracy, there is little danger of what its critics fear – the slide into world government. Let us now turn to this.

WORLD GOVERNMENT

Ideas of world government have a very long history, as Heater's book *World Citizenship and Government* amply demonstrates (Heater 1996). Such ideas were aired in connection with the Roman Empire and, later, the Holy Roman Empire; Dante, the Italian poet, wrote a treatise on the subject in the fourteenth century and it was an idea entertained by some of the irenist thinkers in the Renaissance and Enlightenment as a solution to the quest for 'perpetual peace' ('irene' means 'peace'). Indeed, in the first half of the twentieth century, when ideas of world federalism flourished, much of the concern was with creating the conditions of world peace. In 1946, the World Movement for World Federal Government (WMWFG) was formed and this later became the World Federal Movement, still active today with 25,000 members from over 40 countries. In the second half of the twentieth century, two changes took place in the thinking of the many linked movements. First, as Heater puts it, there was a move from a maximalist advocacy of a fully-fledged world state to a minimalist position of advocating strengthening co-operative measures and the UN – but still wanting us to move from the current international order of sovereign states to a much more integrated world political order in which, for instance, international law can be properly enforced (Heater 1996). Second, the range of concerns broadened to include things like world poverty, the environment and human rights.

Arguments for world government

The following statement of the American-based World Federalist Association indicates current thinking:

The goal of the World Federalist Association is the abolition of war, the preservation of a liveable and healthful global environment, and the promotion of a just world community through the development of enforceable world law. Achievement of that goal requires the establishment of a democratic federal world government with powers adequate to [the goal] [. . .]

In such a federation, international conflicts would be resolved by political and judicial means rather than by violence, while national governments would continue to manage their own internal affairs. World-level crimes would be defined by statute, and persons who broke those laws would be tried and punished by world criminal courts. (World Federalist Association 2002)

The argument is that, in order to achieve these familiar goals, we need some form of world government. As Nielsen argues, we need a world government as a global *Leviathan* to give us peace. Only then, with a coercive world power capable of enforcing compliance to rules, will states have the security they need (Nielsen 1988). Although international law already contains many of the appropriate laws to do with human rights, the environment and so on, it remains ineffective and largely unimplemented (where it conflicts with national interests) because, as Cohen argues, it lacks the authority that comes from decisions being enforceable (Cohen 1954). Only with world government ensuring that others co-operate in self-denying behaviour, will we get over the compliance problem of international relations, particularly over effective environmental restraint. Social justice in relation to meeting the needs of the poor could be effectively implemented, both because the bureaucracy to deliver global 'welfare state' measures would be in place and because the measures could be financed through international taxation (Nielsen 1988).

Arguments against world government

Whilst few global citizens, or indeed thinking people generally, would, of course, dissent from the goals specified, the opposition to world government stems from questioning the connection between world government and these goals. Is world government necessary to achieve these goals? Is it counterproductive in the sense that these very goals may, in some ways, be thwarted? Does it conflict with other values or put at risk other values we also accept?

First, opposition to world government is not the same as a conservative support for the standard conception of international order as order maintained by a society of states. Many global transformations are taking place that are challenging the existing paradigms. This is leading to a 'post-Westphalian' world, as Linklater puts it in *The Transformation of Political*

Community – a world no longer functioning according to the norms of the society of states as largely agreed at the Peace of Westphalia in 1648 (Linklater 1998). New patterns of power and influence are emerging – some to be welcomed, some not – in which global civil society and corporate economic agents will have new roles to play and new relationships to states.

Second, world government would not guarantee universal peace any more than national governments guarantee peace within their borders. Wars would become global civil wars and civil wars are, in many ways, even worse because of divided loyalties. More fundamentally, what needs to be done is to challenge the Hobbesian assumption made by Nielsen and others that peace can only be maintained and strengthened by fear and coercion, and argue that the habits of peace can be developed in various other ways (Jenkins 1973). If world government is based on coercion, it simply replicates at global level the existing pattern of state power and governance. If real progress is to be made in the world, it should be based on less reliance on such methods of achieving peace. The effective implementation of international law is, of course, vital but its authority does not have to depend on a coercive power to enforce implementation. The compliance problem needs to be tackled but through the strengthening of the range of social sanctions, world public opinion and so on.

Third, the danger of world government is that it would become a global tyranny able to suppress human rights without redress and with no effective countervailing force to oppose it. Not only might political rights be eroded, a whole range of civil rights might be undermined too. Many advocates of world government, such as Nielsen, are keen to stress the compatibility of world government with democratic institutions and argue for some form of world federalism in which semi-autonomous regions (no longer fully sovereign, of course, in the traditional sense) each contribute in a democratic way to the decisions made at a global level (Nielsen 1988). But it is difficult to see how this could be guaranteed. Likewise, although a plurality of values could be maintained (Cohen 1954), as it does within modern pluralistic societies, there is a danger that it might not, partly because the analogy is not exact. As it is now, other states and organisations in other states can apply pressures and there are other places where one can escape.

Fourth, adequate measures to tackle evils such as world poverty will only come about if sufficient people believe in the arguments for greater aid, trade reform and so on, and therefore influence governments into taking more action. A radical conception of social distributive justice such as Nielsen's would either *have* to be imposed (if not generally accepted) or would not *need* to be imposed (if it was generally accepted). In short, world government would only be desirable when it became unnecessary.

This is not to discredit the idealism of those world citizens who embrace world federalism, to distance oneself from their ideals or to disagree with many of their practical proposals for strengthening international law, for democratising the United Nations, for supporting the introduction of the International Criminal Court and so on. Clearly, if a world federal order were to be achieved, then we would all be, in a robust sense, global citizens and clearly current global citizens who advocate world federalism have a very strong aspirational aspect to their understanding of global citizenship. There is nothing, however, in the idea of global citizenship that commits us to world federalism. Such a conception of global citizenship is but one of a number of conceptions that are possible.

QUESTIONS

1. What is global governance?
2. Does the existence of the United Nations make us global citizens?
3. What are the attractions of global democracy?
4. Would you join a world federalist organisation?

PART III

THEORETICAL ISSUES

8. CRITIQUE OF THE GLOBAL

SUMMARY OF KEY POINTS COVERED IN THIS CHAPTER

Two challenges to global ethics
  Relativism
  Communitarianism
Critique of relativism
  Strong form: problem of internal dissent and attitude to other cultures
  Weak form: value of some diversity to be recognised
Critique of communitarianism
  Strong form: problem of lack of critique
  Weak form: valuable, especially if extended to the world
Cultural imperialism and ethical agendas
  Danger of Western/Enlightenment projection of values
  Different types of global ethics
  Recognition of the universalist element in all global ethics
  Earth Charter: a test case
  Global ethics as shared values distinguished from global ethics as theories
Realism in international relations
  Realism and internationalism as supported by scepticism about global ethics
  Realism and internationalism as consistent with global ethics but marginalising it
  Positions, both descriptive and normative, challenged by global civil society
Different global ethics
  Many variation in global ethics consistent with global citizenship
  The challenges of ethical minimalism and libertarianism answered
Cosmopolitanism and the value of political community
  Special relationships: rival accounts
  Values of political community: rival accounts
The Nussbaum debate
  Cosmopolitanism or patriotism?
  Combination: cosmopolitan patriotism
  Concentric circles: different interpretations

In this and the final chapter, we take a more critical look at the claims made about global citizenship. Three elements were earlier identified in the basic idea of global citizenship: a *normative* claim about universal values and norms, along with a claim about personal responsibility; an *existential* claim about what forms of institutional or related embodiment exist in the world; and an *aspirational* claim that changes ought to take place in the world to make the realisation of basic values more extensive. In this chapter, we look at the arguments against the normative claim and replies that can be given to them, and in the following chapter the other two claims are critically examined. As Heater notes, there have been two collections (Hutchings and Dannreuther 1999; Cohen 1996) that cover many of the critical issues (Heater 2000; see also Dower 2002b for a condensed assessment of the arguments for and against).

The basic normative claim is discussed in two ways: consideration of an outright rejection of a global ethic underlying it and consideration of the claim that, even if there are cosmopolitan or global values, they have to take second place to the more pressing claims of local community or bounded citizenship.

No Global Ethic?

Relativism and communitarianism

Moral values, on a relativist view, are relative to cultures or societies. They may vary from culture to culture. If cultures have similar values then this is an accident or a reflection of responding to similar needs in similar ways, not because there are universal values which can be objectively discerned (for example, Wong 1984). Linked to this there is an approach to ethics called communitarianism, which stresses that moral values and norms arise out of the shared life of a community and its traditions: obligations are primarily between members of the same community (for example, Sandel 1982; Taylor 1989). Relativism is usually seen as denying the universality of values, whereas communitarianism is concerned with limiting the extent of one's obligations towards others, namely to others in one's society.

In strong forms, both these approaches undermine the claims of global ethics underlying global citizenship. If there are no universal values, the global citizen's assumption that there are is simply mistaken and their behaviour is based on a mistake (rather like a religious person's life being based on a mistake from the point of view of an atheist). If there are no obligations across societal borders, then the global responsibilities active global citizens assume and recommend to others are based on an erroneous understanding of where obligations come from. However, relativism and communitarianism are rarely held nowadays in such a strong form. What is more commonly held is that many but not all moral values are relative to cultures and different, and that whilst most obligations – certainly obligations of a stronger kind – arise from relationships within a society, not all do and some level of global obligation can be accepted. Whether or not these more modest claims are consistent with global citizenship depends both on how the claims are understood and on what kind of global ethic global citizenship is taken to involve. Initially, in the discussion that follows, I assume the stronger forms for the sake of sharpening up the issues.

Critique of relativism

Traditionally, relativism has two aspects: a descriptive claim and a normative claim. The descriptive claim is that, as a matter of fact, there are no universal values, values that are accepted in all cultures; the normative claim is that what is right or good is determined by the practices of the relevant society.

The descriptive claim, though initially very plausible, is, in fact, controversial. It is reasonable to suppose that in all societies there is a core of central values and norms – values such as sustenance, pleasure, freedom from pain, friendship, relationships, community and so on, and norms such as telling the truth, not stealing, not killing others, respect for others (at least as *general* – rather than strictly universal – rules and as pertaining to members of one's own society). We saw in Chapter 2 how thinkers like Küng sought to identify commonalities in all the major religions. Others can argue that any society has to have certain core values and norms in order to function as a society at all. This comes with an important qualification: there are many different expressions of these core values, so it may superficially appear that there is real diversity. For instance, burying and cremating may seem like different customs but they both express fundamentally a norm of respecting the dead.

For some global citizens, it is important that they accept at least a core of universally held values – otherwise, promoting universal values looks like cultural imperialism (see below). By 'universally held' I mean 'by all societies at least, even if not by all individuals', since there will always be a few individuals with unorthodox views! But it is not necessary to believe in such universally held values to be a global citizen and global citizenship is not usually premised on denying the descriptive claim. A global citizen may claim that universal values and norms are not those that are universally held but those values and norms that *ought to be accepted*, or what it would be reasonable to accept. In other words, his ethical theory leads him to assert these values and norms. Furthermore, a third thinker may claim that, even if there are *some* core values and norms that are generally accepted, there are others that are not – like, for instance, respecting nature or cherishing religious diversity – but that are important to promote and part of his goal is to get more people to accept them and act on them! So this takes us to the *normative* claim of relativism, which is the key claim anyway.

The normative claim is that values are determined by particular cultures. There are at least two main problems with this position. First, it makes out a society to be a monolithic whole with one set of agreed norms and values incapable of being challenged in the name of reform or progress by dissenting minorities. On this view, no sense can be made of a minority view that an *accepted* practice *is not right*, for example, on an issue like slavery in the eighteenth century and this is deeply counter-intuitive. Once the plurality of cultural groups within a society is admitted, with a variety of values held, a simple appeal to what is accepted will not do. Second, it provides no principled basis for interaction with other societies. Although relativists often claim it as a merit of their position that one key norm they assert is that of respecting and not interfering with other societies, there is, in fact, a dilemma here. Either the norm of non-interference is a universal principle and therefore not relative, or it is not. If it is not, then there is no more reason for a relativist to accept that principle than its converse, which is not tolerating the outsider. In fact, we generally do, at the very least, accept some norms of inter-societal relations, such as non-interference (other things being equal), coming to the aid of others who suffer and not deliberately attacking others if not provoked. As Apel noted, relativism has no principled basis for condemning the con-quistadors' treatment of the Aztecs, whereas someone who believes in universal human dignity or in some normatively relevant features of *all* human beings *as such* has (Apel 1992; see also Borchert and Stewart 1986). A global citizen then need not be embarrassed by the mere fact that he holds ethical views that are not universally accepted (see also 'ethical agendas' below).

Often relativists have a more modest goal and that is to claim that not all values are universal; that even if we accept that there are common core values and norms and that there are some universal norms governing inter-societal relationship, there is nevertheless a great deal of variation in the ways people live their lives and in the social codes they live by, and there is no reason why one group of people should seek to impose the values and norms particular to their society on other societies. With this normative position many global citizens would agree, whether they call themselves relativist in this sense or prefer another way of supporting the principle of respecting diversity. The idea of respecting diversity of cultures and lifestyles as a key ethical value is certainly not the monopoly of relativism. If one element of human well-being is living according to one's received cultural values, then good reasons drawn from both liberalism and Aristotelianism can be given for protecting cultural diversity (including minority languages as repositories of particular cultures). Liberalism here is understood as asserting the importance of individual *and group* liberty, and Aristotelianism as asserting cultural expression as one universal element of human flourishing.

Critique of communitarianism

Communitarianism has been a very popular position in social and political philosophy in recent years and I can hardly do justice here to a highly nuanced and rich body of thought. It was a reaction to what was perceived to be the rather formal and abstract doctrines of liberalism. Moral agents are not abstract individuals acting on universal principles but situated in concrete communities of shared practices. In many ways, this perspective is important and right. Its problems arise if it is seen as the *whole story* about moral obligation and if it is seen as denying global responsibility but, in fact, the approach can be developed to embrace a more global perspective.

First, the shared traditions of a society might include generosity towards strangers or foreigners (visiting one's country or outside it) – though, equally, they might not and from a communitarian point of view nothing by way of criticism could be made of that. So this point by itself does not take us very far.

Second, granted that obligations arise from actual social relations, practices and traditions, a communitarian need not claim that they exist for no other reason than that tradition and practice has made them so, and can accept that there must be some good or benefit that comes from them. But recognising this leads to recognising that those goods may be achieved in new ways, that some practices may cease to generate them and that similar goods for people not in our society may give rise to obligations as well.

Third, often there is no one community to which people belong but a number of different communities. This is not merely the point that we live in pluralistic multi-cultural societies or nation-states, but that, for many people, amongst the significant communities they belong to are communities of shared concerns that cross national borders and are not defined in terms of territorial space. There are many transnational communities of either particularist solidarities or cosmopolitan solidarities (Scholte 2000), as well as the international community of people acting within the society of states and others acting as agents within the institutions of the global economy. Apart from these transnational communities involving limited numbers of people, it is plausible to say that a wider global moral community is emerging – not, of course, made up of all people but made up of larger numbers of people from all over the world who see themselves as part of a world community that shares at least some common values and norms. As we have seen, the *Universal Declaration of Human Rights* provides the normative framework for such a community, as do other, more recent statements, like the idea of a global civil ethic presented by the Commission on Global Governance and the *Earth Charter*.

Whilst the above account shows that communitarianism need not be opposed to global ethics or global community and thus a global citizen might well understood her global ethic in this way, many others would prefer other ways of understanding and justifying their ethic. For someone who accepts a more traditional grounding for her global ethic in some religious or philosophical truths, the facts about the development of global communities provide not so much the justification of a global ethic as the context in which it can be more effectively expressed. Furthermore, communitarian considerations play an important role in another important debate concerning the relative strengths of communitarian obligations within society and cosmopolitan obligations (see 'The Challenge of Relative Weight' below).

Cultural imperialism

Although the arguments against there being a global ethic as a basis of global citizenship can be answered, there remains a concern that the ethical ideas associated with global citizenship are tainted by cultural imperialism. Cosmopolitanism and global ethics represent an attempt to impose the values of a particular culture on the rest of the world, with the implication that the values emanating from those who assert global values are superior to those of other peoples. Although the criticism is often made in connection with the pursuit of foreign policy in the name of global or universal values, for example in Vietnam, it can also be made about what others, like NGOs or concerned individuals, do in the name of global values. Much recent concern amongst the so-called anti-globalisers about the model of development being promoted in the global economy is about the destruction of local cultures or 'the homogenisation of cultures'. Zolo, for instance has an all-out attack on cosmopolitan agendas, not least human rights thinking, as representing Western ideas emanating from the Enlightenment (Zolo 1997).

Many thinkers are suspicious of the word 'global' in global ethics and global citizenship for similar reasons. This is partly because the word 'global' is associated with the word 'globalisation', with all the latter's negative connotations, and partly because it represents the Enlightenment idea that there is one universal point of view. There is a preference for terms like 'transworld' or 'transnational', which escape these negative connotations. With regard to this preference, we need to be clear whether or not this is just another way of saying 'global' and of referring to universal or shared values under another label. If so, it seems preferable to use the word directly and defend it against the substantive charges.

Do global values *have* to emanate from and reflect a particular cultural background of Western thought? We need to distinguish between values such as respecting diversity, helping others in need, not harming others, not deceiving others, playing one's part in the pursuit of common goods, or respecting rights to liberty, subsistence and security, and more specific values relating to a particular culture or religion (for example, those promoted by missionaries in nineteenth-century Africa or the conquistadors in the Americas). All people have reason to want social life to be conducted according to rules of the former kind. Rights, in particular, like those of the *Universal Declaration of Human Rights*, are generally seen as universally applicable and not a cultural imposition. Such rights are sometimes rejected as not really universal but it not clear why, if some latitude is given to the ways in which rights are realised in particular social contexts, such rights cannot be genuinely universal. Again, the values implicit in the global market economy are sometimes seen as values transcending their origins and genuinely acceptable to people from many different cultural and religious backgrounds and then again sometimes seen as specific and to be rejected. Generally, the validity of the accusation of imperialism depends upon whether one thinks values that are being marginalised or suppressed by a dominant value system *should not be*. The mere fact that a group has minority views does not make the erosion of their views in the name of other values wrong or imperialistic. If dominant moral values eroded the minority views of a racist group or a paedophile ring, few would regard this as culturally imperialistic.

Ethical agendas

The above illustrates how different thinkers will draw the line in different ways between those forms of global ethics they see as genuinely universal and those they see as culturally specific but presented and promoted as global values for all. But this variation should not deflect us from seeing that the distinction is important, since nearly all thinkers draw a line somewhere and do so reasonably. This line is not a line drawn between an unacceptable global ethic with a particular moral agenda, which its adherents want to promote amongst those who do not accept it, and an acceptable global ethic that does not do this because it commands general acceptance anyway.

First, it is doubtful that there is any global ethic in the second sense. Even though some kind of global community is emerging, it is certainly not one in which all thinking people accept the same core values. Second, it is a feature of any global ethic, whether accepted by a large number of people who see themselves as part of large transworld community (like the humanitarian agency networks) or by individuals, that those who believe it promote it as well and try and get others to accept it because, from their point of view, it is right, reasonable or to-be-accepted by all anyway. Any global ethic has an ethical agenda in this sense. Anyone who says that global ethics should not have agendas in this sense contradicts himself, since that 'should' indicates his agenda. A good modern example of a global ethic that does not, on the face of it, represent a form of cultural imposition is the *Earth Charter* (Chapter 6). It is neither universally accepted, since its advocates use it to promote its values through education and persuasion, nor generally regarded as culturally imperialistic, since its values reflect a wide variety of backgrounds and its formulation resulted from a very wide consultation process.

A key issue, already raised in Chapter 5, is: what is it that is being put forward as the global ethic? A set of values and norms or a complete ethical theory, story or worldview? To the extent that what is being promoted is a particular worldview, then the issue of cultural imposition and proselytising comes up (and if the group promoting it is dominant, it would be called imperialism or hegemony), since it is an attempt to get people with other worldviews to abandon their worldview for another, like converting people of one religion to another. To the extent that the values and norms promoted are seen as values and norms that, whilst supported by their promoter's own worldview, are seen as potentially acceptable to others who have other worldviews, then it does not seem unreasonable to seek convergence on those values and norms and try to persuade others to accept them where others do not accept them. If convergence is not achieved (or even attempted where people have radically different values), then there is either partial adjustment and accommodation or conflicts of various kinds. The latter possibility has to be accepted, since the actual norms and values accepted may lead to different policies and hence practical conflict. (This issue is taken up again in Chapter 9 when I discuss responses to September 11th.)

Realism and internationalism

As we have seen in Chapters 5 and 7, two approaches to international relations – realism and internationalism – usually involve an ethical approach that, in one way or another, conflicts with the way a global citizen thinks about global ethics. Here we briefly evaluate critically the arguments for these positions. (For a fuller analysis see Beitz 1979; Dower 1998.)

First, in so far as these positions are consistent with, and indeed motivated by, scepticism about universal values, their advocates see themselves as denying the very thing asserted in global ethics. Thus, a sceptical realist (international sceptic, Hobbesian, anarchist) may deny that ethical norms apply to international relations, partly on the basis of ethical relativism and partly on the basis of the view (associated with Hobbes) that in the absence of any common power to enforce rules, sovereign states live in a moral vacuum: 'where there is no common power, there is no law; where there is no law, no injustice' (Hobbes 1991: 90). A fortiori there are no moral relations between people in different states. Likewise, the internationalist who does believe that there are moral relations between states, may take it that these moral norms of international relations are the product of agreements and conventions that arise between states in their need to get on with each other, and that this is partly in response to the absence of agreed norms in different societies. The problem is to find the bases of international order in the face of political pluralism. On this view again, there is no common global ethic to appeal to.

Second, realism and internationalism do not have to be premised on the absence of a global ethic and generally are not nowadays. Realism can rather be premised on the fact that, in an insecure world of distrustful, autonomous states, 'reasons of state' nearly always trump ethical ideals that would only be followed if they were permitted by or furthered national interests. Likewise, in the internationalist tradition, the moral rules accepted for relations between states may be justified by reference to common moral values (like the natural law in the seventeenth century) but, in practice, this endorses the rights of states to pursue national interests within the rules of mutual respect for sovereignty.

More to the point, in either case, although a universal moral framework is accepted in the background, this does not give individuals any real basis for criticising states for not pursuing policies that pay more attention to moral objectives like distant poverty, human rights violations elsewhere and so on, since, for the reasons given above, states are justified in not doing so. In other words, although global citizens might act themselves and urge other individuals to act to help make a better world, there is no moral propriety in assessing, criticising or pressing governments as part of their ethical commitment. Since such a role is an important part of what makes individuals global *citizens*, through participating (and having a right to participate) in governance, the effect of these two approaches is to marginalise a global ethic, even if it is accepted.

In so far as realist arguments rely on a general scepticism about universal ethics, we have already critically assessed them (under relativism and communitarianism). The specific Hobbesian argument raises further issues, like why does morality depend on enforceability? It is not clear that it does. The duties of individuals do not depend on the fact that those actions can be enforced by laws backed by effective sanctions. States are no different in this regard, though the greater power of some may tempt their representatives to think otherwise.

The realist argument that national interests generally trump moral goals, whilst it does describe what often happens, hardly provides a justification of what happens. If we distinguish between what a state might legitimately do when its security is really threatened from what a state does to promote its interests, it is very implausible to suppose that it has a moral right always to put its interests ahead of those of other states, *given that a universal ethic is accepted*. In parallel, an individual may have a right to self-defence if he is threatened but that does not mean that generally he has a right to put his interests ahead of those of others.

If the internationalist derives the morality of states from the fact that this morality serves the goals of universal morality best, then it is implausible on empirical grounds to claim that respecting sovereignty and maintaining the conditions of international order is all that should be done. Indeed, in recent years, those who defend the internationalist view of international relations are increasingly sensitive to a wide range of goals to do with the environment, poverty and human rights, and also recognise the role of individuals in influencing what happens in world affairs.

Furthermore, realist and internationalist arguments that make national interests a priority over wider moral goals are likely to be weakened from within, in so far as national interests are a function of what citizens, especially acting as electorates, want. If citizens are increasingly motivated by global concerns, then cosmopolitan goals enter domestic policy in that way and people can be effective global citizens by being effective globally-oriented citizens of their own states.

Different global ethics

In the course of this book I have given many examples of global citizenship in action and from these it is apparent that there are core global values that most active global citizens are agreed on. These include substantive values such as peace, care for the environment, tackling poverty, responding to refugees and addressing human rights violations, as well as procedural values such as dialogue and participation. Even if someone tackles one area, he probably broadly approves of people tackling the other areas. There are disagreements on tactics, both about the effectiveness and about the morality of the means taken (Chapter 5). There are also disagreements about other areas as well. Some may advocate pacifism, others not; some be against abortion, others for it; some care for nature for its own sake, others not. Some will have an additional commitment to spread a particular faith, others will resolutely avoid any such further agendas. None of these differences provide any reason for saying a person adopting any of these normative positions is not a global citizen. Indeed, individual global citizens may have profound disagreements with one another. In this respect, they are no different from two people being active citizens within their own state.

It is beyond the scope of this book to evaluate all the arguments for and against particular normative positions that can be taken up. We need, however, to consider one kind of argument because, if it is right, it undermines a distinctive feature of the kind of global ethic typically accepted by a global citizen. It does not undermine the idea of a global ethic *as such* but a particular kind of global ethic I identified earlier as a global ethic of responsibility. This is one in which people take responsibility for the indirect effects of their actions and respond to non-immediate calls on their help. There are at least two sources of resistance to such an ethic. One is a conventionalist theory of morality based on moral convention or mutual agreements that we have duties not to harm one another but no duty to aid one another (Harman 1977). This 'minimalist' kind of morality provides the basis of social order without putting too many demands on one another. Another approach which supports this general idea is 'libertarianism', which stresses that, beyond not invading other people's liberty, we are only required to do what we agree freely to do (Nozick 1974). Thus, if other generally suffer through no fault of mine, I am not obliged to intervene (though I might, out of charity, do so when confronted with it). On this view, we have rights but the duties corresponding to them are duties not to deprive people of their rights, not duties to protect or to aid (contrast Shue's account earlier). Such an ethic would still be a global ethic in the sense of a universal ethic but it would lack precisely the element that characterises the global ethic of a global citizen.

This approach involves a very thin notion of morality and community. Any genuine commitment to membership of a society to which one belongs must lead to having some concern for the conditions in which human well-being is generally achieved. Even if morality were based only on agreement (which it is not), it would surely include a duty to protect and aid as well as a duty not to harm. In relation to the libertarian conception, it is difficult to see how, if liberty is seen as such a central value that we have a duty to respect, we do not have a duty to create or protect the conditions of *effective* liberty. This involves taking active measures for the good of others. I do not have effective liberty if I cannot exercise it for fear of suppression or because I lack the means to exercise it. That said, it remain a vexed question just how far we are required to take positive action for the good of others. As Rawls once remarked, one has a duty to further justice at least at no great cost to oneself (Rawls 1971: 115). Likewise, Shue remarked that, in respect to duties to help alleviate poverty, doing whatever would be needed as one's share *if* everyone did their share is too little; doing everything one can is too much (Shue 1996b: 129). But the issue of how much we should do in relation to global goals is further complicated by the fact that such duties seem to come into conflict with other kinds of duty that arise in one's own community. To that issue I now turn.

THE CHALLENGE OF RELATIVE WEIGHT

What is the issue?

Many people distance themselves from cosmopolitanism or the idea of global citizenship because they take it that this commits them to giving priority to whatever is in the interests of humanity as a whole. If all human beings have moral equality and national boundaries have no moral significance, then it is wrong to give special preference to personal or social relationships in one's own country or to the interests of one's country. However, this is generally rejected because it is believed that we do have special obligations towards 'particular others', such as family, friends or immediate social communities, as well as special obligations as citizens towards the political community we are part of. These obligations compete with, and generally override, any obligations we have towards humanity as a whole.

The insistence on such obligations, many of which arise from membership of communities of particular kinds, might lead one to reject cosmopolitanism as such or it might lead one to accepting it in some modified form, a form that rendered it compatible, for instance, with patriotism. Granted that, in practice, almost everyone accepts that we have a right to devote much attention to pursuing our own well-being, and that we have special relations to family and friends and also to fellow citizens and one's political community, as well as duties to humanity as a whole, there are two substantive issues: (a) what are the relative weightings of these kinds of considerations, especially in the overall balance of a person's decisions about how to use his energy and resources? (b) where ultimately does the source of one's justification come from?

Personal relationships, political community and cosmopolitanism

If one accepts pluralism about the sources of ethics, then it is plausible to say that, for instance, one's duties to family and friends derive from affection, ongoing personal relationships and socially established norms, one's duties to state/wider community from one's membership of an ongoing community with certain traditions, and that if one accepts cosmopolitan duties at all they are to be understood as either a relatively weak 'universal ethic of humanity', or as an aspect of particular norms of one's own moral community (which happen to be open to the outsider, though they might not be), or as newly emerging norms of transnational particularist solidarities or global community. The tendency is for such ways of understanding the 'cosmopolitan' level to make such obligations relatively weak and to provide no moral reasons for wanting to make them stronger.

If, however, one regards one's global ethic as foundational, and as the basic starting point, then the obligations of personal relationships and of political community can still be asserted but given a quite different basis. The cosmopolitan can, in fact, offer one or both of two bases. First, if a global ethic is about promoting the conditions in which a person can lead a good life in the sense of a fully human life, then personal flourishing and special relationships to one's children and to particular others are what it is about. They are elements of the good life. Likewise, participation in community, including political community at any level, is an important part of the universal values to be promoted. (This is a neo-Aristotelian answer.)

Second, the best way in which universal human values are to be promoted is to have and support the existence of particular relationships and sensibilities, including the acceptance of specific duties as secondary applications of the overall goal. Likewise, a cosmopolitan may give as his reason – or at least one of his reasons – the fact that support for human well-being within one's state and support for a properly functioning state are amongst the best means by which human well-being is generally achieved. In any case, in practical terms, it must be accepted that often one's actions are more likely to be effective in one's locality or wider political community than at a distance. Certainly, in respect to two evils of equal badness, one near to hand and one at a distance, efficiency dictates that one attend to what is near. Furthermore, in so far as citizenship is based on various kinds of agreements to co-operate and to accept compliance to laws in return for benefits, the practical value of general duties to honour agreements can be supported. (This is a broadly Utilitarian approach.)

The foundational approach then provides a rather different basis for understanding the role of personal relationships and membership of political communities (and other communities). It is one from which a more radical account of global responsibility can emerge and it can give one a basis for arguing for more extensive obligations, since it requires an answer to the question: are the ways we maintain individual well-being, flourishing personal relationships and a proper relation to one's political community consistent with wider responsibilities to others, including those outside our borders? These considerations incidentally show that arguments for the importance of personal relationships in no way entail the importance of political community. The case for the latter cannot rest on the case for the former. Finding the right balance between these considerations is a complex matter. (Many of the issues have to do with the relative weight of self-concern v. concern for particular others, and of these together v. the claims of one's society and the world taken together, rather than that of society v. the world.) We have only scratched the surface here by providing a framework for thinking about the issues, which the following Nussbaum debate further illustrates.

The Nussbaum debate

In 1994, Martha Nussbaum wrote a lead-article 'Patriotism and Cosmopolitanism' for the *Boston Review*, with a number of replies from various American academics. Her piece was reprinted in 1996 in a book entitled *For Love of Country: Debating the Limits of Patriotism*, together with a revised set of longer responses. This book provides a fascinating insight into the issues I discussed above. I have already indicated Nussbaum's conception of Stoic cosmopolitanism (Chapter 2) and her four main reasons why children should be taught to be global citizens (Chapter 5). Here we consider some of the responses from her American critics. Some reject cosmopolitanism altogether, whilst others feel that it has to be combined with the values of patriotism and communitarian values. One reason for rejecting it is the argument that citizenship requires a corresponding state. Since this is a criticism of the institutional aspect of global citizenship, I consider that further in Chapter 9.

The main thrust of the criticisms are, however, over the implied moral priorities of cosmopolitanism and her claim that it is through seeing ourselves as global citizens that we realise who we really are. For most of the writers, our identity is centrally constituted by various particularities, especially membership of our country. Nussbaum's preference for cosmopolitanism over patriotism, based on her claim that national boundaries are morally irrelevant, is the cause of most resistance. For many, like Barber, it is important to realise that there can be good and bad forms of cosmopolitanism, just as there are good and bad forms of patriotism (Barber 1996: 30). If patriotism is premised on universal values (to be respected in other countries) then it may well be the right basis for education and can be distinguished from a narrow-minded nationalism. Appiah promotes the idea of 'cosmopolitan patriotism' to make this point (Appiah 1996).

Himmelfarb, for instance, remarks 'if nationality, as she says, is "morally irrelevant" to the cosmopolitan ideal, so is the polity that defines the nation, as is the idea of citizenship. And so too is all history' (Himmelfarb 1996: 74). The proposed alternative – cosmopolitanism – is altogether too thin a conception and fails to engage the heart (Barber 1996: 33); Putnam sees it as failing to have any resonance – unlike even describing fellow human beings as 'fellow passengers to the grave' (Putnam 1996: 95). In like manner (not in the book being discussed), MacIntyre once described global citizens as 'rootless citizens of nowhere' (quoted in Almond 1988: 102). What are important to us are our rooted identities.

Nussbaum does not deny these identities. Indeed, she accepts the Stoic idea of concentric circles and remarks:

> We need not give up our special affections and identifications, whether ethnic or gender-based or religious. We need not think of them as superficial, and we may think of our identity as constituted partly by them. We may and should devote special attention to them in education. But we should also work to make all human beings part of our community of dialogue and concern, base our political deliberations on that interlocking commonality, and give the circle that defines our humanity special attention and respect. (Nussbaum 1996: 9)

Here she clearly acknowledges the importance of other circles of identity but sees them as, in some sense, secondary to the circle that defines our humanity. Whilst she does not see special attention and respect as meaning that, in practice, it always has practical priority in our actions, it is this theoretical grounding that is rejected by many of her critics. The implication that we should work towards wider community of dialogue is also rejected because, beyond the existing acceptance of universal framework of human rights and universal values, nothing needs to change in the way Americans think of national identity and patriotism.

Bok, in particular, takes up the challenge of the images of concentric circles. Even if we accept that there are many layers or circles of identity, with corresponding obligations, why should the outermost one have priority? She quotes the nineteenth-century moral philosopher Henry Sidgwick:

> On the one hand he held as a fundamental principle of ethics 'that another's greater good is to be preferred to one's lesser good'. According to this principle, any sacrifice on one's own part would be called for, so long as it could achieve a greater good for others, no matter where they lived. On the other hand, Sidgwick also accepted what he called the common-sense view that our obligations to help others differ depending on the relationships in which we stand to them – relationships of family, friend, neighbour, and fellow citizen. (Bok 1996: 40)

Shue elsewhere links the circles analogy to that of the ripple:

> We often see our duties from the point of view of a pebble dropped in a pond: I am a pebble and the world is the pond I have been dropped into. I am at the centre of a system of concentric circles that become fainter as they spread [. . .] My duties are exactly like the concentric ripples around the pond; strongest at the centre and rapidly diminishing towards the periphery [. . .] my duties to those on the periphery are going to diminish to nothing. (Shue 1988: 691)

As I implied earlier, what is at issue here is not whether we have special obligations to family, friends and neighbours but what the relative importance of obligations are to fellows citizens as opposed to human beings as such. Part of the issue here is simply over how we take the fundamental principle of global ethics. If all human beings have an equal moral status (certainly something Sidgwick would have accepted), then the relative importance of duties to citizens, as opposed to human beings generally, will be dependent on effectiveness and how we justify the special duties of citizenship. Nussbaum's insistence on the special attention to the circle of humanity can be seen as basically a reminder of this fundamental point, not a claim that in practice it always means that distant concerns should take priority over local concerns. Shue's image is not inconsistent with this if it is a *description* of how people think of duty. But as a normative claim it is questionable, since, although in practice my duties are often closer to the centre of my pond because of greater effectiveness, the fact is that I can make a difference to what happens at a distance, particularly if I act in conjunction with others. This is a brute fact of our human condition, particularly in the modern world, so sometimes our duties, about what we ought to do here and now, do relate to what happens at a distance.

Immigration

Our attitudes towards immigration are a good litmus test of how far we adopt cosmopolitan attitudes (Beitz 1983). The issue is not between a completely open immigration policy and one of total refusal to allow immigration. As Wendt notes, even robust cosmopolitans are unlikely to accept a right of free movement across borders (if that includes the right of abode and employment) (Wendt 1999: 131). So long as there are borders and a state system exists, there will be restrictions, though some, like Ottonelli, see moral theory supporting open policies in principle (Ottonelli 2002). The question is: how many restrictions? Global citizens are more inclined to favour generous policies, both for asylum-seekers fleeing persecution and for poor people seeking escape from economic poverty. They allow that the addition of such people may either reduce the average economic benefits of growth enjoyed by existing citizens and residents or even mean that some of the latter are not as well off (because of loss of jobs and so on), and that the social and cultural character of certain areas may be altered. Those with more patriotic or nationalist sentiments are more inclined to resent the sharing of wealth within borders (even though some may support foreign aid) and resent perceived challenges to traditional culture. The issues are complex and emotive.

Concluding remark

The challenge is to find a middle way between two forms of cosmopolitanism, moderate and extreme. As Scheffler puts it in a commentary on the Nussbaum debate, 'Whereas the moderate versions of cosmopolitanism may strike some people as being so obvious as to be platitudinous, the extreme versions may seem so implausible as to be difficult to take seriously' (Scheffler 1999: 262). Almost all people (except the sceptics I considered early in this chapter) accept that we have some duties to distant people but see putting the interests of distant people before self, family, friends and community as absurd. The kind of cosmopolitanism that underlies active global citizenship is, however, one that lies somewhere in the middle between the two extremes. It is nonetheless nearer to the second position than the balance of ethical priorities accepted by most thinkers who resist the label 'cosmopolitan'. We all know that education makes a difference and cosmopolitan education would be no different. The more children know about the world and think about global values, the more they will accept cosmopolitan values and either reject patriotism or interpret it to include cosmopolitan concerns. That is why the traditional patriot and nationalist have reason to resist it. There is a real conflict, even if it is not an 'all or nothing' matter.

QUESTIONS

1. Why might one be sceptical about global values?
2. Why are common theories of international relations a challenge to the idea of global citizenship?
3. What does 'global' in 'global ethics' mean?
4. Can patriotism and cosmopolitanism be combined?

---

9. GLOBAL CITIZENSHIP IN THE WORLD? PRESENT REALITIES AND FUTURE PROSPECTS

SUMMARY OF KEY POINTS COVERED IN THIS CHAPTER

Lack of relevant institutions
  World state required
  Citizenship essentially 'bounded'
  Global obligations and globalisation do not equal global citizenship
  Reply: republican conception applicable globally
Global citizenship is a universal conception, so not applicable if some are
    not global citizens
  Self-description not generally accepted
  Many do not have rights recognised or observed
  Many do not have opportunity for engagement
  Who are active global citizens? Contested issue
Facts about institutions not relevant
  Global citizenship purely ethical
  Global civil society not conceptually necessary, only as means
  Global citizenship as aspiration, not current reality
Aspirational element summarised
  Strengthening global civil society
  Responsibility and respect for diversity
Objections to institutional development
  Preference for world government
  No institutional change needed: matter of moral will
  Opposition from realism
  Replies: real transnational space available and necessary for effective agency
Objections to moral agenda
  No common core
  Reply: need for convergence over wide but not full range of views
  Responses to September 11th: different conceptions of security and
    global priorities

First, we critically assess the claim that we are *now* global citizens in the world both because we all enjoy the status of bearing human rights in international law and because of the real possibility of active engagement in global civil society and global governance. In the second half, the aspirational elements are stated, criticism of the aspirational claim on realist, internationalist and other grounds is itself critically assessed and, finally, different moral agendas for change are compared.

How Things Are

The existential claim summarised

In the course of this book I have identified what I take to be currently existing elements of global citizenship in virtue of which we can say that being a global citizen is more than merely accepting a moral claim about responsibility. These can be summarised as:

> The status of all individuals as subject to international law and in particular bearers of human rights as legal claims;
>
> International institutions, especially the UN and its organs, which provide a concrete institutional embodiment of the values central to global citizenship;
>
> Global civil society, as a vast network of organisations with various global causes (NGOs, churches, to some extent business organisations), including organisations within particular states and the more informal networks of communication (through the Internet and so on);
>
> The opportunities for voluntary engagement by individuals as 'active' global citizens in global concerns through the above organisations and networks (and also national political parties);
>
> Moral community – not a universal community but a matrix of transnational communities of people who see themselves as sharing certain values and working together in solidarity for these values.

This is the existential component of my conception. It is intended to be inclusive: the various elements all contribute to it. Some might prefer us to select from these and thus make rights *or* NGOs *or* moral community the key element. Whilst what I say has a bearing on this issue (and much more could be said), I focus on two more radical criticisms. First, none of these facts is sufficient to establish global citizenship, since rather more needs to exist, such as a world state. Second, none of these facts is necessary for global citizenship, since global citizenship can be seen as essentially an ethical conception, or an ethical conception combined with an aspiration to create the conditions of global citizenship in the future. These criticisms stem at heart from those who have different conceptions of global citizenship and can come from those who think that we are now global citizens but mean something different, and those who think we are not. (The latter may think it is desirable or undesirable that we become global citizens in the future.)

The elements not sufficient

First, these elements do not establish the propriety of talking of global citizenship. None of these are sufficient to amount to *citizenship*. A bald statement of this comes from Michael Walzer, who, in response to Nassbaum's position (discussed in earlier chapters), states:

> I am not a citizen of the world, as she would like me to be. I am not even aware that there is a world such that one could be a citizen of it. No one has ever offered me citizenship, or described the naturalisation processes or enlisted me in the world's institutional structures, or given me an account of its decision procedures (I hope they are democratic), or provided me with a list of the benefits and obligations of citizenship. (Walzer 1996: 125)

A more developed argument for the same general conclusion is provided by David Miller. We saw in Chapter 3 how he defended the republican conception of citizenship, in which participation in a determinate political community is the heart of citizenship. Citizenship in this sense is a valuable achievement that cannot be reproduced on a global scale: *bounded* political community is essential for the existence of citizenship. Globalisation does not make any difference to this. Thinkers are inclined to combine the facts of globalisation with the assertion of global moral obligations to create the case for global citizenship but a case cannot be made. Certainly, there are global obligations but these do not in themselves make us global citizens. Certainly, globalisation includes the emergence of transnational groupings of people working for such moral concerns but such activity is not to be thought of as the activity of citizens addressing fellow citizens in an attempt to reach decisions all can accept. Such activities are confrontational. The facts of international law do not establish citizenship: human rights are not sufficient to establish citizenship and one might only be tempted to think so if one accepted a too weak, liberal conception of citizenship (discussed in Chapter 3). Miller also criticises Falk's conception of the global citizen as a 'citizen-pilgrim' on the grounds that this is really an oxymoron, since a citizen, in having a specific and settled relationship to a locality, is not a pilgrim (Miller 1999). It is important to see that Miller's argument is not merely a legalistic one: he does not claim, as Neff more straightforwardly does, that citizenship requires a formal state in relation to which one has legally defined rights and duties (Neff 1999). This richer account of citizenship, in terms of a more complex attitude towards the state, rules out the idea of global citizenship as truly coherent.

The denial that we are currently global citizens does not, however, have to come from someone who is opposed to the idea as either incoherent or undesirable. It could also come from someone who actually values the idea of global citizenship and thinks that global citizenship depends precisely on creating new institutions in the world in order to make it possible. Such a person might be an advocate of world government or a new form of world federal structure or, more modestly, an advocate of new institutions falling short of world government that constitute some form of cosmopolitan democracy. Either way, for us to be citizens of the world we need to have some formal relationship to world institutions, such as a world state or a world organisation, in which one could democratically participate, for example through elected representatives. These do not exist now, so we are not now world citizens (except in a limited ethical sense), but we could become so one day and, for many, this would be desirable too (van den Anker 2002). (People with such aspirations need not deny the applicability of global citizenship now: see below.)

The arguments for and against world government, and indeed cosmopolitan democracy, were considered in Chapter 7. What is at issue here is more of a conceptual issue: does the *idea* of global citizenship presuppose the existence of global institutions that simply do not exist at present? If so, whether one is a critic or one is an enthusiast, global citizenship simply does not exist.

We can reply to Miller's arguments as follows (Dower 2000). First, even if one just focuses on rights, it is not obvious that rights are not an important aspect of citizenship. Anyone accepting the liberal conception can stress this as an important aspect and therefore, following Marshall's approach, could say we are global citizens in virtue of rights (and duties) in international law. But this would be too quick a reply because it concedes what is after all an important part of citizenship – namely active participation for the public good – as not being relevant to global citizenship. Arguably, that is what people involved in global civil society are precisely doing, albeit in the absence of a formal democratic framework for getting their ideas heard. Is such a person working for global change a citizen-pilgrim? The idea is actually richly suggestive rather than formally contradictory, since it combines some of the elements of bounded citizenship with some of the elements of the pilgrim of no fixed territory in quest of some higher ideal.

Our idea of global citizenship may not be entirely drawn from elements of the present notion of national citizenship but in some ways extends them. The image of a non-territorial agent working through informal networks may well be an aspect of the newly developing conception. In one experiment in extending citizenship beyond national borders, namely European Union citizenship, there is arguably a changing basis for thinking about the bonds of citizenship. As Føllesdal argues, whereas citizenship in the past may have depended more on shared traditions, European citizenship is more based on a shared conception of justice (Føllesdal 2002). (The question whether the UN provides a formal basis for global citizenship was considered in Chapter 7.)

Global citizenship lacks universal application

Here I consider a cluster of arguments (mainly drawn from discussions with students) that question whether we can really talk of *any* of us being global citizens if it is not the case that all of us are. The argument rests on the thought that global citizenship is a universal category. Whatever else it is, global citizenship is a moral conception involving membership of a universal moral community.

First, most people simply do not think of themselves as global citizens. How can a description apply universally when most people do not accept it? Surely, global citizenship is the kind of concept that requires self-ascription as a condition of its applicability. Second, in so far as global citizenship involves the assertion of universal human rights, the fact is that many people in the world do not enjoy human rights in countries where such rights are either not recognised officially or not properly protected. Third, although it may seem plausible to say that the plethora of organisations that now exist make it possible for anyone who so wishes to choose to become an active global citizen, the fact is that many people, especially in poorer countries, simply do not have the means, abilities or opportunities for such engagement. Global citizenship is elitist in being available to rich educated elites, mainly in rich countries. Fourth, global citizenship is not a universal category because there are those who, by their actions, disqualify themselves from being global citizens, such as international terrorists or racists.

Such moves might be made with one of two possible arguments in mind. First, given these facts, what follows is that only some people are global citizens, not all people – only those who describe themselves so, those who do have their human rights actually protected, or those who can join organisations with a view to engagement. Such a move is possible, of course, but it robs the idea of global citizenship of one of its motivating powers – universality. Second, more dramatically, what follows is that none of us are really global citizens, precisely because not all of us are or can be. Because it is an 'all or nothing' concept, its not being applicable to all means it is applicable to none. This means that those who invoke the idea or say they are global citizens are, in some sense, confused or merely using it in another, weaker sense of asserting moral responsibility.

How should one reply to these moves? Can someone be a global citizen without knowing it? Piet Hein, a Danish poet, once said about forty years ago: 'We are global citizens with tribal souls' (quoted in Barnaby 1988: 192). He had in mind the fact that we have responsibilities on a global scale and contribute to global problems whether we realise it or not. Equally, we can say that human beings have human rights or an equal moral status whether we realise it or not. The status of being a global citizen is not an optional one but a consequence of our human nature and condition. The truth or otherwise of these claims is not dependent on whether everyone believes them or not. Of course the status of someone as an active global citizen – someone who, in seeing herself as a global citizen, decides to take action, maybe a lot, maybe a little – applies to only some because that is an optional status, subject to choice.

Someone might reply that the status of having universal rights and duties simply does not amount to a claim about global citizenship (this was part of Miller's position too). Appeal to global citizenship is redundant altogether if we are concerned with moral rights and responsibilities. Many powerful moral arguments for helping others in the world make no reference to global citizenship. The famous example I discussed earlier of Singer's robust principle of helping to prevent evils makes no reference to global citizenship. This must be granted. The theory of global citizenship does not claim that global moral responsibility has to be thought of by agents in global citizenship terms. Rather it interprets the basic facts about moral rights and responsibilities in terms of membership of a global moral community. Furthermore, even if other elements of global citizenship mentioned at the beginning of the chapter are denied or regarded as irrelevant, it still seems advantageous to think of global moral responsibility in terms of global citizenship rather than unadorned moral claims, simply because the implications of membership of a community and of solidarity are likely to be helpful for motivation.

This leads to the more important issue. Does the fact that not everyone enjoys the protection of human rights and not everyone has the possibility of real engagement undermine the universality of global citizenship (as something more substantial than membership of a moral community)? This hardly follows. Human rights as part of international law provide a universal framework. If countries do not formally acknowledge it or fail to observe or allow its violation to occur unchecked, this is deeply regrettable but it does not alter the status, only the effective enjoyment of the status. Likewise, within a country, certain legal rights may simply not be uniformly protected, groups may suffer discrimination and so on, even if those rights are accepted and accepted as rights of citizenship.

The issue of opportunity for active engagement is more complex. Clearly, real opportunity can be limited, if not through lack of resources or ability, through political repression and denial of rights to engage in active politics.

These limitations do not amount to restricting active global citizenship to elites but they do point to a perennial challenge for any democratic culture – how to make such participation more possible for larger proportions of the population. The fact that not everyone can, for financial or psychological reasons, let alone will, become active global citizens is no more an argument against the category than the similar fact about citizens within a country. It can hardly be denied that with the proliferation of NGOs in global civil society (and even more so in respect to networks on the Internet) there are bodies catering for virtually every significant political or ethical position (as well as, of course, every pastime or preference, however weird or evil). Almost anyone with sufficient interest in a global issue can find the organisation of her choice to join up with. Thus, we are all, in principle, global citizens in virtue of the existence of this vast matrix of networks and associations making up the global community, which we can, in principle, link up with. The fact that most people do not do so does not alter the significance of the status we all enjoy in principle.

What about the argument that not all human beings are global citizens because they disqualify themselves by their actions and attitudes? What might we say about a terrorist or a racist? The questions once came up in a class whether bin Laden could be seen as a global citizen, given what he did (assuming he masterminded the September 11th atrocities). We had no idea whether he would have welcomed such a label but the class was divided precisely because he clearly had a global vision and mission although his actions fell outside the range of activities one would regard as the actions of *citizens*. Generally, ardent fanatics ruthlessly pursue ideals without moral restraint. A racist rejects a global ethic of equality of all human beings, though he may have some kind of distorted vision. Could a racist or a fanatic be a global citizen? Our doubts might centre on their rejection of non-violent dialogue, reasoned disagreement, negotiation and actions appropriate to citizenship, and/or their adoption of a vision that is not really a global ethic.

This is an important and complex issue but it does not affect the main point. All such people are, whatever they do, believe or advocate, global citizens in the fundamental sense. They are human beings with certain rights and duties. Nothing they do changes that. If a terrorist commits crimes against humanity, he is liable under international law even if he rejects the authority of that law. Could such people become self-consciously global citizens and active global citizens? To be an *active* global citizen it is necessary that one adopts a global perspective and one acts in the light of it. Is that sufficient? We could take the broad view and say 'yes' and allow the terrorist or fanatic to be global citizens but if we did we would probably add that they were *bad* global citizens and that we reject those forms of global citizenship. But we might equally say that they do not count as global citizens at all because what they stand for and the methods they use are beyond certain limits. Whether one says certain people are not active global citizens or merely active global citizens one rejects, the important point is that the phrase 'active global citizen' is a normatively loaded phrase. The presumption, unless it is explicitly cancelled, is that in calling people (active) global citizens, one is approving of them qua acting as global citizens. This presumption does not mean one approves of what they actually do or think. I have stressed earlier that not all global citizens sing from the same songsheet. Even if one disagrees with the rightness or effectiveness of chosen means, or even with chosen goals if reasonably pursued, one still approves of the engagement in public affairs – the same is true of citizenship itself.

Where one draws the line between acceptable and welcome forms of active global citizenship and what is not varies from thinker to thinker. Some approaches are more inclusive over the range of views that are acceptable (as I have recommended), some less so. Global citizenship is, in these respects, a contested concept – what we count as authentic global citizenship depends on our values, though it does not affect the claim that, at a basic level, we are *all* global citizens. It is generally better that more people are active global citizens with a wide range of views. Since a vibrant civil society is bound to be one in which there is a wide variety of means taken and ends pursued, one may welcome the activities of groups whose tactics one disagrees with as part of a positive manifestation of global concern. (A culture that allows the expression of even extremist views is more likely to encourage the critical development of global perspectives that are progressive than one in which they are suppressed.)

Facts about institutions and so on are not relevant to global citizenship

The argument hitherto has been that certain factors about the world as it is are not sufficient to establish the category 'global citizen'; what we now consider is a rival approach that says they are not necessary. To say they are not necessary is to say either that they are not *conceptually* necessary (not essential to its meaning) or that they are not *empirically* necessary (not causally needed in order to achieve what global citizens want).

If we say that the existence of institutions of global civil society or other aspects of global community are not conceptually necessary, we mean that global citizenship does not *mean* involvement in these. The simplest understanding would be one that is quite common: that global citizenship does not mean anything more that a belief in a global ethic and a commitment to make the world a better place. This is a purely ethical interpretation of the phrase.

If someone chooses to use the term 'global citizen' to mean merely the ethical conception, one may have to accept that as another meaning of the phrase. Certainly, many people so use it. Nevertheless, it is a less adequate conception precisely because it empties the term 'citizen' of any real conceptual work to be done. If membership of a moral community is included, then that idea of membership is captured by the 'citizen' element – but it does not amount to much compared with the other elements I have discussed.

Now someone with an ethical conception may well, in practice, use all sorts of ways of promoting ethical agendas that involve precisely the factors I have mentioned – human rights law, institutions, NGOs and other parts of global civil society. Does that mean she implicitly does accept the institutional component? Not really. There is a difference between using the institutions of global civil society as an effective means to one's moral ends and seeing these same institutions as constitutive of global citizenship. If these institutions are means, they are externally related to citizenship; if they are constitutive, they are internal to it. However, it is more plausible to argue that they are internal to it. Then we make more sense of the 'citizenship' component, since it has more conceptual work to do and, in talking, as it is natural to do, of such institutions as *embodiment* of global citizenship, we make better sense of the relationship between the moral commitments of agents and what they characteristically use to express these concerns. In like manner, F. H. Bradley, the nineteenth-century political theorist, suggested that we think of morality having both a body and a soul – the body being public institutions, rules and practices, and the soul the private moral wills of individuals who breathe life into those institutions (Bradley 1876: 177–81).

A more complex ethical interpretation is one that combines a global vision of a future world in which we were global citizens in a fully institutional sense with a commitment to work towards it. A world federalist would identify with this case; for him, the current institutions do not make us global citizens but those of us who aspire to create them can be called 'global citizens' in an aspirational sense. We might have what H. G. Wells called a 'mental cosmopolis' that precedes the actual cosmopolis of the future (quoted in Heater 1996: 129). Likewise, someone who thinks that we need a formal cosmopolitan democracy can say we are not global citizens now except in an aspirational sense. (In fact, advocates of cosmopolitan democracy need not deny, and generally accept, that current global civil society or informal democratic elements make us global citizens now, albeit in a less full sense.)

With regard to someone who sees global citizenship as a current aspirational commitment to creating an appropriate institutional framework for global citizenship in the full sense sometime in the future, my difficulty with this is not that it contains an aspirational element. Indeed, that is an important dimension. It is rather that what is proposed is either not essential (cosmopolitan democracy) or not appropriate (world government) as the 'institutional' component for global citizenship and also that, if the current state of the world is not seen as providing already at least some kind of institutional embodiment to citizenship, then the conception is wedded to a largely conventional and legalistic conception of citizenship. It also has the consequence that, as things stand, only a few people are global citizens because they have chosen to work for these goals – even those in the rest of global civil society are not really global citizens because they have other goals. This seems too restrictive.

I said earlier that an advocate of a purely ethical conception of global citizenship might go further than the conceptual point but also make the empirical point that global citizenship simply does not require the institutional apparatus I have outlined above. There are things one can do that do not involve institutions; there are different kinds of activities other than public actions, like prayer; there are other ways of understanding community, such as a spiritual or metaphysical community. Stoic cosmopolitanism often had the latter otherworldliness to it. Whilst few global citizens today would eschew the use of what is available in the world of global institutions and networks (including churches themselves, which are highly globalised), what I have just mentioned is a reminder that these institutions may be seen sometimes as external means and sometimes as inappropriate.

The Way Forward

The aspirational claim restated

I suggested at the beginning of this book that global citizenship has an aspirational component – anyone believing in global citizenship has some view about what needs to change in the world. For some, it may be an important part of their thinking (as with world federalists) but for others it may be relatively unimportant part, perhaps only a belief that the world ought to become one in which certain core values come to be both more generally accepted and also acted upon. For some, the institutions that constitute global citizenship may be already in place and what we need to do is to strengthen them in the future in the service of global goals; for others, what we are precisely aiming for in the future, using what institutions we have now, is the creation of the conditions of true global citizenship. Different conceptions will interpret the aspirational element very differently.

To summarise points made throughout this book, I see my own aspirational component as follows. It has two parts, one institutional, the other normative. Institutionally, whilst what exists is adequate for global citizenship to have application as the world is now, various institutions need to be strengthened: human rights law needs to be strengthened and more effectively implemented, which includes the development of the duties of individuals in international law (as illustrated by moves to establish an International Criminal Court); global civil society needs to expand but, more particularly, various ways in which individuals and groups within it connect with what governments, international institutions and global economic institutions do need to evolve;

global democracy must develop and we must achieve the transformation of democratic politics within countries through the increasing importance of global concerns amongst the concerns of citizens and political activists. Normatively, the kind of global ethic I hope global citizens would come increasingly to accept is one that combines responsibility with respect for diversity of both customs and worldviews, that seeks convergence where beliefs initially clash, that rejects the norms of sceptical realism and inter-nationalism and that increasingly relies on the way of peace, non-violence, dialogue and appeal to law as opposed to relying on violence and the threat of violence.

Objections to the institutional programme

Objections to my outline of institutional development might stem from at least three sources, two from rival conceptions of global citizenship and one from a perspective lying outside it. First, there is the objection that it does not go far enough. What we need is a world in which cosmopolitan democracy is formally instituted, or a world federal order. Whilst I welcome the develop-ment of the former, provided safeguards are in place to keep it from sliding into world government, I have already indicated reasons for being unhappy with the latter. Second, there is the objection that it goes too far. The current arrangements in the world are quite adequate: if things are not going well enough, it is because of lack of moral will, not inadequacies in institutional arrangements. Third, thinkers from traditional backgrounds in politics and international relations may resist further incursions into their dominance and influence, even regretting changes that have already taken place.

The idea that the way forward to a world that is more humane, just, peaceful and kind to the environment is through increasing adherence to existing codes of moral conduct is an attractive one in many ways. If only we would act more on the basic moral rules that are generally accepted, then real change would take place without any more developments in global civil society, global governance, human rights law and so on. Much of the emphasis in the work of the USA-based Institute for Global Ethics is on getting people, particularly in public life and business, to become 'ethically fitter' and more willing to put basic values into practice (Institute for Global Ethics 2002). The Moral Rearmament Movement was premised on similar ideas. Interest in corporate responsibility in business (linked to interest in corporate global citizenship) is also based on the idea that businesses can behave responsibly in the world if its officers act to higher moral standards. All this is fine. However, the private moral wills of individuals need both empowerment through institutions and reinforcement from laws and regula-tions, and the protection of rights is better achieved where compliance is not left to private conscience. If the moral values we wish to see extended include the acceptance of the global scope of obligation, it is particularly important that there is a global culture that is given its character by the institutions in it, the meetings that take place within it and the public documents that emerge from them.

Another source of resistance to strengthening the institutions of global citizenship comes from traditional thinking in international relations and politics. This resistance is part of a general resistance to globalisation. In short, the world is still to be seen as a Westphalian system in which states exercise power within their own borders and govern the world between them through international co-operation in the society of states. This exercise of power and governance is both descriptive and normative. Descriptively, this is how it happens and there is no real space in which individuals, even acting through global organisations, have any real influence, except at the edges. Normatively, this is how it ought to be, since the values we cherish – such as democracy, security and justice – are more likely to be achieved, on balance, in such a political and international order than through the development of multipolar patterns of influence. We have already had reason to comment on this kind of approach (Chapter 7), so I will only add here that, whilst it is helpful to be reminded that states and their multilateral agreements and laws remain dominant forces in global affairs, we are turning the clock back if we try and halt or reverse the trends we have noted.

The facts are that there is a glaring democratic deficit, that there are massive global problems that states still locked into competing agendas are not tackling all that well, and that organisations within global civil society do already exert quite lot of influence in various ways, such as framing international law. To argue normatively that individuals should not exploit the social spaces emerging in order to influence global agendas is to try and exclude a powerful force for the good (Linklater 1999). In any case, the extent to which countries will pursue more globally enlightened agendas is a function of what their electorates want or feel ought to be priorities. The development of these global agendas cannot just happen within national borders – it is essentially a transnational process requiring transnational expression.

The moral agenda

The kind of moral agenda I have developed in this book and which I believe to be what many (though by no means all) global citizens would endorse is one in which the core human values of security, justice and democracy are to be achieved not merely through the agency of governments within a society of states but also through global responsibility exercised by individuals to support these goals and through the acceptance of respect for diversity. This is an approach I have called solidarist pluralism, though an easier label might be an ethic of responsibility and respect for diversity (Dower 1998).

At one level, this might seem rather obvious and uncontroversial. Do not almost all thinkers, whether they think of themselves as global citizens or not, subscribe to these core values, though they might put less emphasis upon global responsibility and respect for diversity? Thus, a realist defender of the central role of nation-states and the international system argues that the best way to protect values is to have a strong state system and stable international order. Those centrally involved as drivers of the global economy see neo-liberal values as the key to prosperity for all, which will in the long run achieve the three core values more effectively than other approaches. Those who subscribe to a particular religious worldview may support these core values, though they generally have other ethical and religious values that they think important to promote as well.

One of the chief challenges facing us in the early twenty-first century is finding a common core of global values around which we can unite, whatever our particular background in terms of culture and belief. The seminal work *Our Global Neighbourhood* (CGG 1995) stresses, as we saw in Chapter 2, the need to find a 'global civic ethic' as an important aspect of tackling global problems – an emphasis not so apparent in early documents of this kind. The *Earth Charter* is another ambitious attempt to provide a basis for general acceptance. In so far as global citizenship is linked to the idea of a global community, the idea of a community does at least presuppose, if not the existence now, at least the emergence in the future of a set shared values underlying such a community.

The task of finding a real common core is daunting. I have already stressed during this book that, even if we focus on those who would call themselves global citizens, there are significant differences of approach. But there is an even larger amount of variation in the ways people think about global issues, if we include those who are not self-described global citizens and work out what their global values are and how they apply them or recommend application of them. Apart from disagreements about the effectiveness and rightness of the means, people have very different theories and worldviews – religious or philosophical – that they bring to the justification of whatever global ethic they endorse. What do we make of these facts?

Generally, we need to recognise them, not pretend that differences do not exist; we also need to approach such difference in a non-confrontational and dialogical way. However, the key issue is: what do we do about differences of worldview? One of the advantages of the kind of ethic I have advocated is that it seeks to find agreement on core values *where agreement is possible* without making an issue of the fact that people come with very different religious and philosophical worldviews. This is the recognition that what is important and realistic is finding agreement about core values and practical policies, rather than trying to get others to accept one's own worldviews, which is not important and certainly not realistic. The latter is a prescription for conflict and even wars in the future.

It might be thought that the kind of view I have advocated – of global responsibility and respect for diversity, including diversity of worldview – is not actually an approach that will minimise conflict in the world. It is just another view that competes with other kinds of global ethic. Its very minimalism in not making any one complete worldview important precisely makes it a competitor with other positions. A whole range of thinkers who support, for instance, the global economy, the current international order, or indeed any religious or philosophical position in which the specific worldview is important to the thinker, may take issue with it. This difficulty is reinforced if we remember that others have uncompromising ethical agendas – in particular, the terrorist, the fanatic or even the hard-nosed realist who rejects the global point of view.

If this is so, then the prospects for the future are not great and the attempts to identify or create a shared global ethic – shared generally, not universally, since universal acceptance is an unrealistic pipedream – are doomed to failure. My own view is that there are real possibilities of convergence between those who support and work within the global economy, those who support and work within the international system and those who come with particular worldviews based on their religious or cultural backgrounds. Worldviews and the ethics they endorse are not as inflexible as they are often thought. Accommodations are possible. Although, to some, my approach may seem to be just another view in the ring and thus to be opposed, I submit that it represents the possibility of convergence. An example of some current significance is that of the relation between secular liberalism and Islam. It is often said that they are deeply antagonistic and that what we see emerging is a clash of civilisations (Huntington 1996). This is not, however, the only interpretation that can be made. Islam is not, it has often been said, against capitalism and is itself, at least amongst many of its adherents, committed to the toleration of diversity. Accommodation with terrorists, fanatics and extreme realists is less realistic, of course. The challenge here is twofold: how in the shorter term to contain what they do and how to create a future world in which these approaches are less likely to be taken up. There is a tension between these goals – a tension illustrated by responses to September 11th which, to be frank, dents my general optimism about the possibility of convergence of core values.

September 11th

What happened on 11 September 2001 illustrates well the nature of modern global problems. The attack on the twin towers of the World Trade Center by two hijacked aeroplanes and the crashing into the Pentagon by a third demonstrated in all too vivid a fashion the global nature of terrorism. Terrorism is not global because it occurs in all parts of the world, it is global because it is conducted by agents from other parts of the world, often as part of networks spread across the world; because the targets were not just American – the people killed were and would have been predicted to be from many different countries; and because the attack was not just against America but global capitalism itself. The response led by America has been a 'global war against terrorism'. Nominally, it has been a war supported by a large coalition of countries set to deal with the common global goal of getting rid of terrorism. Terrorism is a global problem either because it is an evil that has to be eliminated or severely reduced, or because, in addition to that problem, the attempt to deal with it by military action is exacerbating many other problems in the world.

It has sometimes been said that the events of 11 September 2001 changed the world but in what ways is very unclear. At one level, it has certainly changed how the USA is engaging with the world in its war against terrorism. But at another level, the events might lead to changing the whole way we think about security, creating a more secure world in which international law can become a vehicle for dealing with terrorist crimes against humanity. That these things have not yet happened suggests that perhaps very little will change. What concerns me about this is both a substantive issue as to whether the war against terrorism is right or appropriate and also how far, if terrorism is to be tackled in this way, it marginalises the role of individuals acting in global civil society in trying to create a better world – militaristic solutions are authoritarian rather than democratic. The voices of peace and justice for all are not being heard very much, though there has been a high level of response from global civil society in the form of vigils, marches, writing and so on. The reason why this issue challenges my plea for and expectation of convergence is that there appears to be considerable divergence between the responses and attitudes of the key governments involved and those of many active global citizens. It is not that there is disagreement about the goal: trying to reduce terrorism is right. The disagreement is over both the priority given to *one* goal, the methods adopted and the mindset involved.

At the heart of the issue I am raising is: what do we mean by security? Or rather: what aspects of security do we regard as having priority? The war against terrorism is premised on one very small aspect of security – being secure from terrorist attacks. Even if this goal were fully achievable (which is extremely unlikely and certainly not by war, which will create more terrorists), its being a priority makes other aspects of security less important – environmental security, economic security (not being extremely poor) and greater personal security within societies. They are rendered less important because more energy and resources go into this one objective, with consequent deflection from other humanitarian purposes; furthermore, many of these other values are actually jeopardised by the particular ways in which the goal is being pursued by war.

What is missing is a recognition that, if the threat of terrorism is to be reduced, and if other core vales in the world are to be effectively addressed as well, many other things need to be done and emphasised: tackling the root causes of the global inequalities that fuel extremists; tackling the militarisation of the world; tackling the perception of a clash of civilisations; challenging the resort to war as the primary response, as opposed to seeing terrorism as an international crime that needs to be dealt with by due legal process at the international level. Even if we just focus on security itself as a core value, and emphasise its range and importance *for all people*, trying to create a global order that meets security needs requires new ways of thinking (Dower 2002a).

I do not wish to suggest that all global citizens agree with my doubts about the rightness of the current strategy to deal with international terrorism. I am sure many – perhaps with reluctance – accept what is being done. However, I do regard the emergence of active engagement in world affairs by individuals, whatever their views, as a positive development pointing to the emergence of a world that will be less dominated by the aggressive pursuit of national interests and a narrow interpretation of security. A groundswell of active concern is likely to develop in favour of at least the following: the protection of the full range of human goods; effective human rights law and international law generally in defence of their status as human goods; and democratic engagement in global affairs, since global affairs now affect us all. It is these concerns and the right to have them heard that seem to me to be questioned by the current responses to September 11th. It is, of course, too soon to know how things will change in the longer term. These events remind us how difficult the achievement of acceptable convergence is. They do not really undermine the importance of global citizenship. Given what is at stake – a more humane, just and peaceful world – they render it all the more important.

QUESTIONS

1. Does it make sense to say that only some people are global citizens?
2. Why, if at all, is global civil society important for global citizenship?
3. When you think of the future of the world, what kinds of changes are most important to you?
4. How do you think the events of September 11th have changed global priorities?

The reader might also like to reconsider the Questions in Chapter 1 and explore whether his or her answers are now any different.

APPENDIX I
UNIVERSAL DECLARATION
OF HUMAN RIGHTS

ADOPTED AND PROCLAIMED BY GENERAL ASSEMBLY
RESOLUTION 217 A (III) OF 10 DECEMBER 1948

On 10 December 1948 the General Assembly of the United Nations adopted and proclaimed the *Universal Declaration of Human Rights*, the full text of which appears in the following pages. Following this historic act, the Assembly called upon all Member countries to publicize the text of the Declaration and 'to cause it to be disseminated, displayed, read and expounded principally in schools and other educational institutions, without distinction based on the political status of countries or territories'.

PREAMBLE

Whereas recognition of the inherent dignity and of the equal and inalienable rights of all members of the human family is the foundation of freedom, justice and peace in the world,

Whereas disregard and contempt for human rights have resulted in barbarous acts which have outraged the conscience of mankind, and the advent of a world in which human beings shall enjoy freedom of speech and belief and freedom from fear and want has been proclaimed as the highest aspiration of the common people,

Whereas it is essential, if man is not to be compelled to have recourse, as a last resort, to rebellion against tyranny and oppression, that human rights should be protected by the rule of law,

Whereas it is essential to promote the development of friendly relations between nations,

Whereas the peoples of the United Nations have in the Charter reaffirmed their faith in fundamental human rights, in the dignity and worth of the human person and in the equal rights of men and women and have determined to promote social progress and better standards of life in larger freedom,

Whereas Member States have pledged themselves to achieve, in co-operation with the United Nations, the promotion of universal respect for and observance of human rights and fundamental freedoms,

Whereas a common understanding of these rights and freedoms is of the greatest importance for the full realization of this pledge,

Now, Therefore THE GENERAL ASSEMBLY proclaims THIS UNIVERSAL DECLARATION OF HUMAN RIGHTS as a common standard of achievement for all peoples and all nations, to the end that every individual and every organ of society, keeping this Declaration constantly in mind, shall strive by teaching and education to promote respect for these rights and freedoms and by progressive measures, national and international, to secure their universal and effective recognition and observance, both among the peoples of Member States themselves and among the peoples of territories under their jurisdiction.

Article 1

All human beings are born free and equal in dignity and rights. They are endowed with reason and conscience and should act towards one another in a spirit of brotherhood.

Article 2

Everyone is entitled to all the rights and freedoms set forth in this Declaration, without distinction of any kind, such as race, colour, sex, language, religion, political or other opinion, national or social origin, property, birth or other status. Furthermore, no distinction shall be made on the basis of the political, jurisdictional or international status of the country or territory to which a person belongs, whether it be independent, trust, non-self-governing or under any other limitation of sovereignty.

Article 3

Everyone has the right to life, liberty and security of person.

Article 4

No one shall be held in slavery or servitude; slavery and the slave trade shall be prohibited in all their forms.

Article 5

No one shall be subjected to torture or to cruel, inhuman or degrading treatment or punishment.

Article 6

Everyone has the right to recognition everywhere as a person before the law.

Article 7

All are equal before the law and are entitled without any discrimination to equal protection of the law. All are entitled to equal protection against any discrimination in violation of this Declaration and against any incitement to such discrimination.

Article 8

Everyone has the right to an effective remedy by the competent national tribunals for acts violating the fundamental rights granted him by the constitution or by law.

Article 9

No one shall be subjected to arbitrary arrest, detention or exile.

Article 10

Everyone is entitled in full equality to a fair and public hearing by an independent and impartial tribunal, in the determination of his rights and obligations and of any criminal charge against him.

Article 11

(1) Everyone charged with a penal offence has the right to be presumed innocent until proved guilty according to law in a public trial at which he has had all the guarantees necessary for his defence.
(2) No one shall be held guilty of any penal offence on account of any act or omission which did not constitute a penal offence, under national or international law, at the time when it was committed. Nor shall a heavier penalty be imposed than the one that was applicable at the time the penal offence was committed.

Article 12

No one shall be subjected to arbitrary interference with his privacy, family, home or correspondence, nor to attacks upon his honour and reputation. Everyone has the right to the protection of the law against such interference or attacks.

Article 13

(1) Everyone has the right to freedom of movement and residence within the borders of each state.
(2) Everyone has the right to leave any country, including his own, and to return to his country.

Article 14

(1) Everyone has the right to seek and to enjoy in other countries asylum from persecution.
(2) This right may not be invoked in the case of prosecutions genuinely arising from non-political crimes or from acts contrary to the purposes and principles of the United Nations.

Article 15

(1) Everyone has the right to a nationality.
(2) No one shall be arbitrarily deprived of his nationality nor denied the right to change his nationality.

Article 16

(1) Men and women of full age, without any limitation due to race, nationality or religion, have the right to marry and to found a family. They are entitled to equal rights as to marriage, during marriage and at its dissolution.
(2) Marriage shall be entered into only with the free and full consent of the intending spouses.
(3) The family is the natural and fundamental group unit of society and is entitled to protection by society and the State.

Article 17

(1) Everyone has the right to own property alone as well as in association with others.
(2) No one shall be arbitrarily deprived of his property.

Article 18

Everyone has the right to freedom of thought, conscience and religion; this right includes freedom to change his religion or belief, and freedom, either alone or in community with others and in public or private, to manifest his religion or belief in teaching, practice, worship and observance.

Article 19

Everyone has the right to freedom of opinion and expression; this right includes freedom to hold opinions without interference and to seek, receive and impart information and ideas through any media and regardless of frontiers.

Article 20

(1) Everyone has the right to freedom of peaceful assembly and association.
(2) No one may be compelled to belong to an association.

Article 21

(1) Everyone has the right to take part in the government of his country, directly or through freely chosen representatives.
(2) Everyone has the right of equal access to public service in his country.
(3) The will of the people shall be the basis of the authority of government; this will shall be expressed in periodic and genuine elections which shall be by universal and equal suffrage and shall be held by secret vote or by equivalent free voting procedures.

Article 22

Everyone, as a member of society, has the right to social security and is entitled to realization, through national effort and international co-operation and in accordance with the organization and resources of each State, of the economic, social and cultural rights indispensable for his dignity and the free development of his personality.

Article 23

(1) Everyone has the right to work, to free choice of employment, to just and favourable conditions of work and to protection against unemployment.
(2) Everyone, without any discrimination, has the right to equal pay for equal work.

(3) Everyone who works has the right to just and favourable remuneration ensuring for himself and his family an existence worthy of human dignity, and supplemented, if necessary, by other means of social protection.

(4) Everyone has the right to form and to join trade unions for the protection of his interests.

Article 24

Everyone has the right to rest and leisure, including reasonable limitation of working hours and periodic holidays with pay.

Article 25

(1) Everyone has the right to a standard of living adequate for the health and well-being of himself and of his family, including food, clothing, housing and medical care and necessary social services, and the right to security in the event of unemployment, sickness, disability, widowhood, old age or other lack of livelihood in circumstances beyond his control.

(2) Motherhood and childhood are entitled to special care and assistance. All children, whether born in or out of wedlock, shall enjoy the same social protection.

Article 26

(1) Everyone has the right to education. Education shall be free, at least in the elementary and fundamental stages. Elementary education shall be compulsory. Technical and professional education shall be made generally available and higher education shall be equally accessible to all on the basis of merit.

(2) Education shall be directed to the full development of the human personality and to the strengthening of respect for human rights and fundamental freedoms. It shall promote understanding, tolerance and friendship among all nations, racial or religious groups, and shall further the activities of the United Nations for the maintenance of peace.

(3) Parents have a prior right to choose the kind of education that shall be given to their children.

Article 27

(1) Everyone has the right freely to participate in the cultural life of the community, to enjoy the arts and to share in scientific advancement and its benefits.

(2) Everyone has the right to the protection of the moral and material interests resulting from any scientific, literary or artistic production of which he is the author.

Article 28

Everyone is entitled to a social and international order in which the rights and freedoms set forth in this Declaration can be fully realized.

Article 29

(1) Everyone has duties to the community in which alone the free and full development of his personality is possible.
(2) In the exercise of his rights and freedoms, everyone shall be subject only to such limitations as are determined by law solely for the purpose of securing due recognition and respect for the rights and freedoms of others and of meeting the just requirements of morality, public order and the general welfare in a democratic society.
(3) These rights and freedoms may in no case be exercised contrary to the purposes and principles of the United Nations.

Article 30

Nothing in this Declaration may be interpreted as implying for any State, group or person any right to engage in any activity or to perform any act aimed at the destruction of any of the rights and freedoms set forth herein.

APPENDIX 2
THE EARTH CHARTER

Adopted by the Earth Council in March 2000

PREAMBLE

We stand at a critical moment in Earth's history, a time when humanity must choose its future. As the world becomes increasingly interdependent and fragile, the future at once holds great peril and great promise. To move forward we must recognize that in the midst of a magnificent diversity of cultures and life forms we are one human family and one Earth community with a common destiny. We must join together to bring forth a sustainable global society founded on respect for nature, universal human rights, economic justice, and a culture of peace. Towards this end, it is imperative that we, the peoples of Earth, declare our responsibility to one another, to the greater community of life, and to future generations.

Earth, Our Home

Humanity is part of a vast evolving universe. Earth, our home, is alive with a unique community of life. The forces of nature make existence a demanding and uncertain adventure, but Earth has provided the conditions essential to life's evolution. The resilience of the community of life and the well-being of humanity depend upon preserving a healthy biosphere with all its ecological systems, a rich variety of plants and animals, fertile soils, pure waters, and clean air. The global environment with its finite resources is a common concern of all peoples. The protection of Earth's vitality, diversity, and beauty is a sacred trust.

The Global Situation

The dominant patterns of production and consumption are causing environmental devastation, the depletion of resources, and a massive extinction of species. Communities are being undermined. The benefits of development are not shared equitably and the gap between rich and poor is widening. Injustice, poverty, ignorance, and violent conflict are widespread and the cause of great suffering. An unprecedented rise in human population has overburdened ecological and social systems. The foundations of global security are threatened. These trends are perilous – but not inevitable.

The Challenges Ahead

The choice is ours: form a global partnership to care for Earth and one another or risk the destruction of ourselves and the diversity of life. Fundamental changes are needed in our values, institutions, and ways of living. We must realize that when basic needs have been met, human development is primarily about being more, not having more. We have the knowledge and technology to provide for all and to reduce our impacts on the environment. The emergence of a global civil society is creating new opportunities to build a democratic and humane world. Our environmental, economic, political, social, and spiritual challenges are interconnected, and together we can forge inclusive solutions.

Universal Responsibility

To realize these aspirations, we must decide to live with a sense of universal responsibility, identifying ourselves with the whole Earth community as well as our local communities. We are at once citizens of different nations and of one world in which the local and global are linked. Everyone shares responsibility for the present and future well-being of the human family and the larger living world. The spirit of human solidarity and kinship with all life is strengthened when we live with reverence for the mystery of being, gratitude for the gift of life, and humility regarding the human place in nature.

We urgently need a shared vision of basic values to provide an ethical foundation for the emerging world community. Therefore, together in hope we affirm the following interdependent principles for a sustainable way of life as a common standard by which the conduct of all individuals, organizations, businesses, governments, and transnational institutions is to be guided and assessed.

PRINCIPLES

I. Respect and care for the community of life

1. *Respect Earth and life in all its diversity*
a. Recognize that all beings are interdependent and every form of life has value regardless of its worth to human beings.
b. Affirm faith in the inherent dignity of all human beings and in the intellectual, artistic, ethical, and spiritual potential of humanity.

2. *Care for the community of life with understanding, compassion, and love*
a. Accept that with the right to own, manage, and use natural resources comes the duty to prevent environmental harm and to protect the rights of people.
b. Affirm that with increased freedom, knowledge, and power comes increased responsibility to promote the common good.

3. *Build democratic societies that are just, participatory, sustainable, and peaceful*
a. Ensure that communities at all levels guarantee human rights and fundamental freedoms and provide everyone an opportunity to realize his or her full potential.
b. Promote social and economic justice, enabling all to achieve a secure and meaningful livelihood that is ecologically responsible.

4. *Secure Earth's bounty and beauty for present and future generations*
a. Recognize that the freedom of action of each generation is qualified by the needs of future generations.
b. Transmit to future generations values, traditions, and institutions that support the long-term flourishing of Earth's human and ecological communities.

In order to fulfill these four broad commitments, it is necessary to:

II. Ecological integrity

5. *Protect and restore the integrity of Earth's ecological systems, with special concern for biological diversity and the natural processes that sustain life*
a. Adopt at all levels sustainable development plans and regulations that make environmental conservation and rehabilitation integral to all development initiatives.

b. Establish and safeguard viable nature and biosphere reserves, including wild lands and marine areas, to protect Earth's life support systems, maintain biodiversity, and preserve our natural heritage.

c. Promote the recovery of endangered species and ecosystems.

d. Control and eradicate non-native or genetically modified organisms harmful to native species and the environment, and prevent introduction of such harmful organisms.

e. Manage the use of renewable resources such as water, soil, forest products, and marine life in ways that do not exceed rates of regeneration and that protect the health of ecosystems.

f. Manage the extraction and use of non-renewable resources such as minerals and fossil fuels in ways that minimize depletion and cause no serious environmental damage.

6. *Prevent harm as the best method of environmental protection and, when knowledge is limited, apply a precautionary approach*

a. Take action to avoid the possibility of serious or irreversible environmental harm even when scientific knowledge is incomplete or inconclusive.

b. Place the burden of proof on those who argue that a proposed activity will not cause significant harm, and make the responsible parties liable for environmental harm.

c. Ensure that decision making addresses the cumulative, long-term, indirect, long distance, and global consequences of human activities.

d. Prevent pollution of any part of the environment and allow no build-up of radioactive, toxic, or other hazardous substances.

e. Avoid military activities damaging to the environment.

7. *Adopt patterns of production, consumption, and reproduction that safeguard Earth's regenerative capacities, human rights, and community well-being*

a. Reduce, reuse, and recycle the materials used in production and consumption systems, and ensure that residual waste can be assimilated by ecological systems.

b. Act with restraint and efficiency when using energy, and rely increasingly on renewable energy sources such as solar and wind.

c. Promote the development, adoption, and equitable transfer of environmentally sound technologies.

d. Internalize the full environmental and social costs of goods and services in the selling price, and enable consumers to identify products that meet the highest social and environmental standards.

e. Ensure universal access to health care that fosters reproductive health and responsible reproduction.

f. Adopt lifestyles that emphasize the quality of life and material sufficiency in a finite world.

8. *Advance the study of ecological sustainability and promote the open exchange and wide application of the knowledge acquired*
a. Support international scientific and technical cooperation on sustainability, with special attention to the needs of developing nations.
b. Recognize and preserve the traditional knowledge and spiritual wisdom in all cultures that contribute to environmental protection and human well-being.
c. Ensure that information of vital importance to human health and environmental protection, including genetic information, remains available in the public domain.

III. Social and economic justice

9. *Eradicate poverty as an ethical, social, and environmental imperative*
a. Guarantee the right to potable water, clean air, food security, uncontaminated soil, shelter, and safe sanitation, allocating the national and international resources required.
b. Empower every human being with the education and resources to secure a sustainable livelihood, and provide social security and safety nets for those who are unable to support themselves.
c. Recognize the ignored, protect the vulnerable, serve those who suffer, and enable them to develop their capacities and to pursue their aspirations.

10. *Ensure that economic activities and institutions at all levels promote human development in an equitable and sustainable manner*
a. Promote the equitable distribution of wealth within nations and among nations.
b. Enhance the intellectual, financial, technical, and social resources of developing nations, and relieve them of onerous international debt.
c. Ensure that all trade supports sustainable resource use, environmental protection, and progressive labor standards.
d. Require multinational corporations and international financial organizations to act transparently in the public good, and hold them accountable for the consequences of their activities.

11. *Affirm gender equality and equity as prerequisites to sustainable development and ensure universal access to education, health care, and economic opportunity*
a. Secure the human rights of women and girls and end all violence against them.
b. Promote the active participation of women in all aspects of economic, political, civil, social, and cultural life as full and equal partners, decision makers, leaders, and beneficiaries.
c. Strengthen families and ensure the safety and loving nurture of all family members.

12. *Uphold the right of all, without discrimination, to a natural and social environment supportive of human dignity, bodily health, and spiritual well-being, with special attention to the rights of indigenous peoples and minorities*
a. Eliminate discrimination in all its forms, such as that based on race, color, sex, sexual orientation, religion, language, and national, ethnic or social origin.
b. Affirm the right of indigenous peoples to their spirituality, knowledge, lands and resources and to their related practice of sustainable livelihoods.
c. Honor and support the young people of our communities, enabling them to fulfil their essential role in creating sustainable societies.
d. Protect and restore outstanding places of cultural and spiritual significance.

IV. Democracy, nonviolence, and peace

13. *Strengthen democratic institutions at all levels, and provide transparency and accountability in governance, inclusive participation in decision making, and access to justice*
a. Uphold the right of everyone to receive clear and timely information on environmental matters and all development plans and activities which are likely to affect them or in which they have an interest.
b. Support local, regional and global civil society, and promote the meaningful participation of all interested individuals and organizations in decision making.
c. Protect the rights to freedom of opinion, expression, peaceful assembly, association, and dissent.
d. Institute effective and efficient access to administrative and independent judicial procedures, including remedies and redress for environmental harm and the threat of such harm.

e. Eliminate corruption in all public and private institutions.

f. Strengthen local communities, enabling them to care for their environments, and assign environmental responsibilities to the levels of government where they can be carried out most effectively.

14. *Integrate into formal education and life-long learning the knowledge, values, and skills needed for a sustainable way of life*

a. Provide all, especially children and youth, with educational opportunities that empower them to contribute actively to sustainable development.

b. Promote the contribution of the arts and humanities as well as the sciences in sustainability education.

c. Enhance the role of the mass media in raising awareness of ecological and social challenges.

d. Recognize the importance of moral and spiritual education for sustainable living.

15. *Treat all living beings with respect and consideration*

a. Prevent cruelty to animals kept in human societies and protect them from suffering.

b. Protect wild animals from methods of hunting, trapping, and fishing that cause extreme, prolonged, or avoidable suffering.

c. Avoid or eliminate to the full extent possible the taking or destruction of non-targeted species.

16. *Promote a culture of tolerance, nonviolence, and peace*

a. Encourage and support mutual understanding, solidarity, and cooperation among all peoples and within and among nations.

b. Implement comprehensive strategies to prevent violent conflict and use collaborative problem solving to manage and resolve environmental conflicts and other disputes.

c. Demilitarize national security systems to the level of a non-provocative defense posture, and convert military resources to peaceful purposes, including ecological restoration.

d. Eliminate nuclear, biological, and toxic weapons and other weapons of mass destruction.

e. Ensure that the use of orbital and outer space supports environmental protection and peace.

f. Recognize that peace is the wholeness created by right relationships with oneself, other persons, other cultures, other life, Earth, and the larger whole of which all are a part.

THE WAY FORWARD

As never before in history, common destiny beckons us to seek a new beginning. Such renewal is the promise of these Earth Charter principles. To fulfill this promise, we must commit ourselves to adopt and promote the values and objectives of the Charter.

This requires a change of mind and heart. It requires a new sense of global interdependence and universal responsibility. We must imaginatively develop and apply the vision of a sustainable way of life locally, nationally, regionally, and globally. Our cultural diversity is a precious heritage and different cultures will find their own distinctive ways to realize the vision. We must deepen and expand the global dialogue that generated the Earth Charter, for we have much to learn from the ongoing collaborative search for truth and wisdom.

Life often involves tensions between important values. This can mean difficult choices. However, we must find ways to harmonize diversity with unity, the exercise of freedom with the common good, short-term objectives with long-term goals. Every individual, family, organization, and community has a vital role to play. The arts, sciences, religions, educational institutions, media, businesses, nongovernmental organizations, and governments are all called to offer creative leadership. The partnership of government, civil society, and business is essential for effective governance.

In order to build a sustainable global community, the nations of the world must renew their commitment to the United Nations, fulfill their obligations under existing international agreements, and support the implementation of Earth Charter principles with an international legally binding instrument on environment and development.

Let ours be a time remembered for the awakening of a new reverence for life, the firm resolve to achieve sustainability, the quickening of the struggle for justice and peace, and the joyful celebration of life.

BIBLIOGRAPHY

Where several chapters are given from the same book, full bibliographical details are given in the book entry. Websites are notorious for changing addresses; if a reader cannot access the one given, she should try typing the name into a search engine.

Aiken, W. and H. LaFollette (eds) (1996), *World Hunger and Morality*, Engelwood Cliffs: Prenticehall.

Alkire, S. (2002), 'Global Citizenship and Common Values', in Dower and Williams (2002).

Almond, B. (1990), 'Alasdair MacIntyre: The Virtue of Tradition', *Journal of Applied Philosophy*, vol. 7, no. 1.

Aman, K. (ed.) (1991), *Ethical Principles for Development: Needs, Capacities and Rights*, Upper Montclair, NJ: Institute for Critical Thinking, Montclair State University.

Amnesty International (February 2002), http://www.amnesty.org/

Apel, K.-O. (1992), 'The moral imperative', *UNESCO Courier*, July/August.

Appiah, K. W. (1996), 'Cosmopolitan Patriots', in Cohen (1996).

Aquinas, T. [c. 1270] (1953), *Summa Theologiae*, excerpts in D. Bigongiari (ed.), *The Political Ideas of St Thomas Aquinas*, New York: Hafner.

Archibugi, D. and D. Held (eds) (1995), *Cosmopolitan Democracy – An Agenda for a New World Order*, Cambridge: Polity Press.

Archibugi, D. (1995), 'From the UN to cosmopolitan democracy' in Archibigi and Held (1995).

Aristotle [c. 350 BC] (1988), *The Politics*, in S. Everson (ed.), Cambridge: Cambridge University Press.

Attfield, R. (1983), *The Ethics of Environmental Concern*, New York: Columbia University Press.

Attfield, R. (1999), *The Ethics of the Global Environment*, Edinburgh: Edinburgh University Press.

Attfield, R. (2002), 'Global Citizenship and the Global Environment', in Dower and Williams (2002).

Augustine [c. 412] (1947), *City of God*, London: Dent.

Axtmann, R. (2002), 'What's Wrong with Cosmopolitan Democracy?', in Dower and Williams (2002).

Bailey, S. (1996), *Peace is a Process*, London: Quaker Home Service.

Barber, B. R. (1996), 'Constitutional Faith', in Cohen (1996).

Barnaby, F. (ed.) (1988), *The Gaia Peace Atlas*, London: Pan Books.

Beitz, C. R. (1979), *Political Theory and International Relations*, Princeton: Princeton University Press.

Beitz, C. R. (1983), 'Cosmopolitan Ideals and National Sentiment', *Journal of Philosophy*, vol. 80, no. 10.

Beitz, C. R. (1999), 'International Liberalism and Distributive Justice: A Survey of Recent Thought', *World Politics*, vol. 51, no. 2.

Beitz, C. R. et al (eds) (1985), *International Ethics*, Princeton: Princeton University Press.

Bok, S. (1996), 'From Part to Whole', in Cohen (1996).

Borchert D. M. and D. Stewart (1986), *Explaining Ethics*, London: Macmillan.

Bradley, F. H. (1876), *Ethical Studies*, Oxford: Oxford University Press.

Bull, H. (1977), *The Anarchical Society*, 1st ed., London: Macmillan.

Carter, A. (2001), *The Political Theory of Global Citizenship*, London: Routledge.

Cicero, (1959), *De Re Publica*, trans. C. W. Keyes, London: Heinemann.

Cohen, J. (1954), *The Principles of World Citizenship*, Oxford: Blackwell.

Cohen, J. (ed.) (1996), *For Love of Country: Debating the Limits of Patriotism* Boston: Beacon Books.

Commission on Global Governance (CGG) (1995), *Our Global Neighbourhood*, Oxford: Oxford University Press.

Council of Europe (1950), *European Convention on Human Rights*, Rome: Council of Europe.

Crocker, D. A. (1991), 'Towards Development Ethics', *World Development*, vol. 19, no. 5.

Crocker, D. A. (1998), *Transitional Justice and International Civil Society*, Working Paper No. 13, University Park, MD: The National Commission on Civic Renewal.

Curle, A. (1981), *True Justice*, London: Quaker Home Service.

Davison, A. (1996), *Technology and the Contested Meanings of Sustainability*, New York: SUNY Press.

des Jardins, J. R. (1997), *Environmental Ethics – An Introduction to Environmental Philosophy*, Belmont, CA: Wadsworth.

Dobson, A. (ed.) (1999), *Fairness and Futurity*, Oxford: Oxford University Press.

Dower, N. and J. Williams (2002), *Global Citizenship: A Critical Reader*, Edinburgh: Edinburgh University Press.

Dower, N. (1995), 'Peace and security: some conceptual notes', in M. Salla et al. (eds), *Essays on Peace*, Rockhampton: Central Queensland University Press.

Dower, N. (1998), *World Ethics – the New Agenda*, Edinburgh: Edinburgh University Press.

Dower, N. (2000), 'The Idea of Global Citizenship – A Sympathetic Assessment', *Global Society*, vol. 14, no. 4.

Dower, N. (2001), 'Does Global Citizenship Require Modern Technology?', *Ends & Means*, vol. 5, no. 2.

Dower, N. (2002a), 'Against War as a Response to Terrorism', *Philosophy and Geography*, vol. 5, no. 1.

Dower, N. (2002b), 'Global Citizenship: Yes or No?', in Dower and Williams (2002).

Dower, N. (2002c), 'Global Ethics and Global Citizenship', in Dower and Williams (2002).

Earth Charter (March 2002), www.earthcharter.org/

Edwards, M. and J. Gaventa (2001), *Global Citizen Action*, London: Earthscan.

Engel, J. R. and J. B. Engel (eds) (1990), *Ethics of Environment and Development: Global Challenges and International Responsibilities*, London: Belhaven Press.

Environmental Investigation Agency (EIA) (March 2002), http://www.eia-international.org/

Ethical Consumer (2002), http://www.ethicalconsumer.org/

Falk, R. (1994), 'The Making of Global Citizenship', in Bart van Steenbergen (ed.), *The Condition of Citizenship*, London: Sage.

Falk, R. (1995), *On Humane Governance: Toward a New Global Politics*, Cambridge: Polity Press.

Falk, R. (2002), 'An Emergent Matrix of Citizenship: Complex, Uneven, and Fluid', in Dower and Williams (2002).

Feinberg, J. (1973), *Social Philosophy*, Engelwood Hills: Prentice-Hall.

Ferguson, J. (1988), *Not Them but Us – In Praise of the United Nations*, East Wittering: Gooday Publishers.

Fishkin, J. (1985), 'The theory of justice and international relations: the limits of liberal theory', in A. Ellis (ed.), *Ethics and International Relations*, Manchester: Manchester University Press.

Føllesdal, A. (2002), 'Citizenship: European and Global', in Dower and Williams (2002).

Gewirth, A. (1978), *Reason and Morality*, Chicago: Chicago University Press.

Gruzalski, B. (2001), *Gandhi*, Belmont, CA: Wadsworth.

Hare, R. M. (1963), *Freedom and Reason*, Oxford: Oxford University Press.

Hare, R. M. (1972), 'Peace', *Applications of Moral Philosophy*, London: Macmillan.

Harman, G. (1977), *The Nature of Morality*, New York: Oxford University Press.

Heater, D. (1996), *World Citizenship and Government: Cosmopolitan Ideas in the History of Western Political Thought*, Basingstoke: Macmillan.

Heater, D. (2000), 'Does Cosmopolitan Thinking have a Future?', *Review of International Studies*, vol. 26.

Heater, D. (2002), *World Citizenship: Cosmopolitan Thinking and its Opponents*, London: Continuum.

Held, D. and A. McGrew (2000), *The Global Transformations Reader*, Cambridge: Polity Press.

Held, D. (1995), *Democracy and the Global Order: From the Modern State to Cosmopolitan Governance*, Cambridge: Polity Press.

Held, D. (1999), 'The Transformation of Political Community: Rethinking Democracy in the Context of Globalisation', in Shapiro and Hacker-Cordon (1999) (reprinted in part in Dower and Williams (2002)).

Himmelfarb, G. (1996), 'The Illusions of Cosmopolitanism', in Cohen (1996).

Hobbes, T. [1651] (1991), *Leviathan*, R. Tuck (ed.), Cambridge: Cambridge University Press.

Human Rights Watch (February 2002): http://www.hrw.org/

Huntington, S. P. (1996), *The Clash of Civilizations and the Remaking of World Order*, New York: Simon and Schuster.

Hutchings, K. and R. Dannreuther (eds) (1999), *Cosmopolitan Citizenship*, Basingstoke: Macmillan.

Hutchings, K. (1999), 'Political Theory and Cosmopolitan Citizenship', in Hutchings and Dannreuther (1999).

Hutchings, K. (2002), 'Feminism and Global Citizenship', in Dower and Williams (2002).

Imber, M. (2002), 'The UN and Global Citizenship', in Dower and Williams (2002).

Institute for Global Ethics (2002), http://www.globalethics.org/

InterAction Council (1997), *A Universal Declaration of Human Responsibilities*, Tokyo.

Isin, F. I. and P. K. Wood (1999), *Citizenship & Identity*, London: Sage.

Jenkins, I. (1973), 'The Conditions of Peace', *The Monist*, vol. 57, no. 4.

Jubilee 2000 UK (March 2002), http://www.jubilee2000uk.org/

Kant, I. [1784] (1970a), *The Idea of a Universal History with a Cosmopolitan Intent*, in H. Reiss (ed.), *Kant's Political Writings*, Cambridge: Cambridge University Press.

Kant, I. [1795] (1970b), *Perpetual Peace*, in H. Reiss (ed.), *Kant's Political Writings*, Cambridge: Cambridge University Press.

Kant, I. [1785] (1949), *The Groundwork of the Metaphysic of Morals*, in H. Paton, (ed.), *The Moral Law* London: Hutchinson.

Khan, S. A. (1996), *Environmental Responsibility: Review of the 1993 TOYNE REPORT*, Department for Education and Employment/Department of Environment/Welsh Office.

Küng, H. (1991), *Global Responsibility – In Search of a New World Ethic*, London: SCM Press.

Küng, H. (2002), 'A Global Ethic for a New World Order', in Dower and Williams (2002).

Küng, H. and K.-J. Kuschel (1993), *A Global Ethic: The Declaration of the Parliament of the World's Religions*, London: SCM Press.

Kymlicka, W. (1999), 'Citizenship in an Era of Globalisation: Comments on Held', in Shapiro and Hacker-Cordon (1999).

Kymlicka, W. (1995), *Multicultural Citizenship*, Oxford: Oxford University Press.

Lackey, D. (1989), *Ethics of War and Peace*, Englewood Cliff: Prentice Hall.

Leopold, A. (1949), *A Sand County Almanac and Sketches Here and There*, Oxford: Oxford University Press.

Linklater, A. (1992), 'What is a Good International Citizen?', in P. Keal (ed.), *Ethics and Foreign Policy*. London: Allen and Unwin.

Linklater, A. (1998), *The Transformation of Political Community: Ethical Foundations of the Post-Westphalian Era*, Cambridge: Polity Press.

Linklater, A. (1999), 'Cosmopolitan Citizenship', in Hutchings and Dannreuther (1999).

Linklater, A. (2002), 'Cosmopolitan Citizenship', in B. Turner and E. Isin (eds), *Citizenship Studies: A Handbook*, London: Sage.

Locke, J. [1689] (1960), *Second Treatise of Government*, in P. Laslett (ed.), Cambridge: Cambridge University Press.

Luard, E. (1979), *The United Nations*, London: Macmillan.

Luard, E. (1981), *Human Rights and Foreign Policy*, London: Pergamon Press.

Luban, D. (1985), 'Just war and human rights', in Beitz (1985).

Mackie, J. L. (1984), 'Can there be a right-based moral theory?', in J. Waldron (ed.), *Theories of Rights*, Oxford: Oxford University Press.

Macnamara, R. (1980), *Address to Board of Governors*, Washington: World Bank.

Macquarrie, J. (1973), *The Concept of Peace*, New York: Harper and Row.

Madely, J. (1982), *Human Rights Begin with Breakfast*, London: Pergamon Press.

Marshall, T. H. (1973), *Class, Citizenship and Social Development*, Westport, CN: Greenwood Press.

McGrew, A. (2000), 'Democracy beyond Borders?', in Held and McGrew (2000).

Médecins Sans Frontières (March 2002), http://www.msf.org/

Mill, J. S. [1861] (1962), *Utilitarianism*, M. Warnock (ed.), London: Fontana.

Miller, D. (1998), 'The Left, the Nations State and Citizenship', *Dissent*, 1998 (reprinted in Dower and Williams (2002).

Miller, D. (1999), 'Bounded Citizenship', in Hutchings and Dannreuther (1999).

Mothersson, K. (1992), *From Hiroshima to the Hague: A Guide to the World Court Project*, Geneva: International Peace Bureau.

Neff, S. C. (1999), 'International Law and the Critique of Global Citizenship', in Hutchings and Dannreuther (1999).

Newlands, D. (2002), 'Economic Globalisation and Global Citizenship', in Dower and Williams (2002).

Nielsen, K. (1988), 'World government, security and social justice', in S. Luper-Foy, (ed.), *Problems of International Justice*.

Nozick, R. (1974), *Anarchy, State and Utopia*, Oxford: Blackwell.

Nussbaum, M. (1996), 'Patriotism and Cosmopolitanism', in Cohen (1996).

O'Neill, O. (1989), *Faces of Hunger*, London: Allen and Unwin.

Ottonelli, V. (2002), 'Immigration: What does Global Justice Require?', in Dower and Williams (2002).

Oxfam (1998), *A Curriculum for Global Citizenship: A Guide for Teachers and Education Workers*, London: Oxfam.

Oxfam (2001), 'Key Principles for an International Educational Entitlement for Global Citizenship', working paper, London: Oxfam.

Parekh, B. (2003), 'Cosmopolitan and Global Citizenship', *Review of International Studies*, vol. 32, no. 1.

Peace Corps (March 2002), www.peacecorps.gov/

Penz, P. (1991), 'The Priority of Basic Needs: Towards a Consensus in Development Ethics for Political Engagement', in Aman (1991).

Pogge, Thomas W. (1992), 'Cosmopolitanism and Sovereignty', *Ethics*, vol. 103.

Putnam, H. (1996), 'Must we Choose between Patriotism and Universal Reason?', in Cohen (1996).

Rawls, J. (1971), *A Theory of Justice*, Oxford: Oxford University Press.

Robertson, R. (1992), *Globalisation: Social Theory and Global Culture*, London: Sage.

Rolston, H. (1988), *Environmental Ethics*, Philadelphia: Temple University Press.

Rousseau, J.-J. [1762] (1966), *The Social Contract*, in G. D. Cole (trans.), London: Dent.

Sandel, M. (1982), *Liberalism and the Limits of Justice*, Cambridge: Cambridge University Press.

Scheffler, S. (1999), 'Conceptions of Cosmopolitanism', *Utilitas*, vol. 11, no. 3.

Scholte, J. A. (2000), *Globalization: A Critical Introduction*, Basingstoke: Palgrave.

Sen, A. (1999), *Development as Freedom*, Oxford: Oxford University Press.

Sen, A. and B. A. O. Williams (eds) (1982), *Utilitarianism and Beyond*, Cambridge: Cambridge University Press.

Shapiro, I. and X. Hacker-Cordon (eds) (1999), *Democracy's Edges*, Cambridge: Cambridge University Press.

Shue, H. (1988), 'Mediating ethics', *Ethics*, vol. 98.

Shue, H. (1996a), *Basic Rights: Subsistence, Affluence and US Foreign Policy*, 2nd ed., Princeton: Princeton University Press.

Shue, H. (1996b), 'Solidarity Among Strangers and the Right to Food', in Aiken and LaFollette (1996).

Sidgwick, H. [1877] (1919), *Elements of Politics*, London: Macmillan.

Singer, P. (1972), 'Famine, affluence and morality', *Philosophy & Public Affairs*, vol. I, and extended in 'Rich and poor', in P. Singer (ed.), *Practical Ethics*, Cambridge: Cambridge University Press.

Slim, H. (1988), 'Sharing a Universal Ethic: The Principle of Humanity in War', *The International Journal of Human Rights*, vol. 2.

Smart, J. C. C. and B. A. O. Williams (1973), *Utilitarianism For and Against*, Cambridge: Cambridge University Press.

Smyth, J. and C. Blackmore (2002), 'Living with the Big Picture: A Systems Approach to Citizenship in a Complex Planet', in Dower and Williams (2002).

Spybey, T. (1996), *Globalization and World Society*, Cambridge: Polity Press.

Strijbos, S. (2002), 'Citizenship in our Globalising World of Technology', in Dower and Williams (2002).

Taylor, C. (1989), *Sources of the Self: The Making of Modern Identity*, Cambridge, MA: Harvard University Press.

Thompson, J. (2001), 'Planetary citizenship: the definition and defence of an ideal', in B. Gleeson and N. Low (eds) (2001), *Governing for the Environment*, Basingstoke: Palgrave.

Tomlinson, J. (1999), *Globalization and Culture*, Cambridge: Polity Press.

Toyne, P. (1993), *Environmental Responsibility: An Agenda for Further and Higher Education*, London: HMSO.

Trident Ploughshares (February 2002), http://www.tridentploughshares.org/

United Nations (1966), *Covenant on Civil and Political Rights*, New York: UN.

United Nations (1966), *Covenant on Social, Economic and Cultural Rights*, New York: UN.

United Nations (1986), *Declaration on the Right to Development*, New York: UN.

United Nations (1989), *Convention on the Rights of the Child*, New York: UN.

United Nations (1994), *Doc HRI*, New York: UN.

van den Anker, C. (2002), 'Global Justice, Global Institutions and Global Citizenship', in Dower and Williams (2002).

van Steenbergen, B. (1994), 'Towards a global ecological citizen', in B. van Steenbergen (ed.), *The Condition of Citizenship*, London: Sage.

Vincent, R. J. (1986), *Human Rights and International Relations*, Cambridge: Cambridge University Press.

von Clausewitz, C. [1832] (1968), *On War*, in A. Rappoport (ed.), Harmondsworth: Penguin Books.

Walzer, M. (1996), 'Spheres of Affection', in Cohen (1996).

Wendt, A. (1999), 'A Comment on Held's Cosmopolitanism', in Shapiro and Hacker-Cordon (1999).

Williams, J. (2002), 'Good International Citizenship', in Dower and Williams (2002).

Wong, D. (1984), *Moral Relativity*, Berkeley: University of California Press.

World Commission on Environment and Development (WCED) (1987), *Our Common Future (The Brundtland Report)*, Oxford: Oxford University Press.

World Court (1996), *Advisory Judgement*, General List No. 95, 8 July.

World Court Project (February 2002), http://www.wcp.gn.apc.org/

World Development Movement (WDM) (March 2002), http://www.wdm.org.uk/

World Federalist Association (March 2002), http://www.wfa.org/

Young, I. (2000), *Inclusion and Democracy*, Oxford: Oxford University Press.

Zolo, D. (1997), *Cosmopolis – Prospects for World Government*, Cambridge: Polity Press.

INDEX